Mike McGrath

Building Android Apps

second edition
covers App Inventor 2

In easy steps is an imprint of In Easy Steps Limited
16 Hamilton Terrace · Leamington Spa
Warwickshire · United Kingdom · CV32 4LY
www.ineasysteps.com

Second Edition

In Easy Steps Limited supports The Forest Stewardship Council (FSC),
the leading international forest certification organization. All our titles
that are printed on Greenpeace approved FSC certified paper carry the
FSC logo.

MIX
Paper from
responsible sources
FSC® C020837

Printed and bound in the United Kingdom

ISBN 978-1-84078-629-3

Contents

Preface

The creation of this book has provided me, Mike McGrath, a welcome opportunity to demonstrate how MIT App Inventor can be easily used to create applications for today's portable devices. All examples I have given in this book demonstrate app features using the current online version of App Inventor 2 hosted by the MIT Center for Mobile Learning.

Conventions in this book

Hello.apk

The examples provide screenshots of the actual App Inventor blocks used to implement each step for clarity. Additionally, in order to identify each example described in the steps, a colored icon and an Android Application Package file name appears in the margin alongside the steps.

Grabbing the source code

For convenience I have placed source code files from the examples featured in this book into a single ZIP archive. You can obtain the complete archive by following these easy steps:

1. Browse to **www.ineasysteps.com** then navigate to Free Resources and choose the Downloads section

2. Find Building Android Apps in easy steps, 2nd Edition in the Downloads list, then click on the hyperlink entitled All Code Examples to download the archive

3. Now, extract the archive contents to any convenient location on your computer – the source code for each example is contained in its own individual AIA archive

4. You may then upload any AIA archive example into App Inventor using the "Import project (.aia) from my computer menu" option on the My Projects page Project menu

Import Project...

| Choose File | Hello.aia |

Cancel   OK

I sincerely hope you enjoy discovering the powerful, exciting possibilities of MIT App Inventor and have as much fun with it as I did in writing this book.

Mike McGrath

1 Getting started

Welcome to the exciting world of application development for Android. This chapter shows how to establish an app development environment and demonstrates how to create a simple Android app.

Introducing Android

Android is an operating system for mobile phones and tablets, in much the same way that Microsoft Windows is an operating system for PCs. The Android operating system is maintained by Google and comes with a range of useful features as standard.

Standard Android features include Google Search and Google Maps, which means you can easily search for information on the web and find directions from your phone – as you would on your computer. This is handy for discovering things like train times and getting directions when out and about. Other Google services, such as Gmail and Google Earth can also be accessed from devices running the Android operating system. You can easily check Facebook and Twitter profiles too, through a variety of applications (apps) – making it ideal for social networking.

There is a huge range of custom apps available to download from the Google Play Store. For example, there are camera apps such as "Camera 360" – that allow you to take photos with artistic effects, and music player apps such as "Winamp" – that allow you to import MP3s and create playlists, and popular game apps, such as "Candy Crush Saga" – that provide great fun entertainment.

Android is an open-source operating system, built on the open-source Linux Kernel, which means it can be easily extended to incorporate new cutting-edge technologies as they emerge. Android was brilliantly designed, from the ground-up, to enable developers to create compelling apps that can fully exploit all the host device's capabilities. For example, an app can access all of a phone's core functionality such as making calls, sending text messages, or taking photos. The Android platform will continue to evolve as the developer community works together to build innovative mobile applications and you can be part of this exciting innovation process with MIT App Inventor 2.

The New icon pictured above indicates a new or enhanced feature introduced in the latest version App Inventor 2.

MIT App Inventor 2

App Inventor enables you to develop applications for Android devices using a web browser and a connected device or a device emulator – without writing a single line of code. It is a web-based tool developed by MIT in which the App Inventor servers store your work and help you keep track of your projects. When the app is finished you can package it to produce an "application package" (Android **.apk** file) that can be shared around and installed on any Android phone or tablet like any other app. App Inventor 2 is supported by a wide range of operating systems and web browsers, with these minimum specifications:

Computer operator system requirements...

● **Windows**: Windows XP, Vista, Windows 7, Windows 8+

● **Linux**: Ubuntu 8+, Debian 5+

● **Mac**: Mac OS X 10.5+

Web browser requirements...

● **Google Chrome**: 4.0+

● **Mozilla Firefox**: 3.6+

● **Apple Safari**: 5.0+

App Inventor 2, which is demonstrated in this book, runs completely in the browser – unlike App Inventor 1, which was demonstrated in the previous edition of this book. This means you can begin building apps online immediately but to test your apps you will need to install one or two pieces of software:

● **MIT AI2 Companion**: for installation on an Android device to enable live testing on that device via a WiFi network

● **aiStarter**: for installation on a computer system to enable the web browser to communicate with an Android device emulator

The procedure of testing apps on an virtual emulator and live testing on a physical device are demonstrated in this chapter.

At the time of writing Microsoft Internet Explorer is not supported by MIT App Inventor 2.

Beginning your first app

The App Inventor 2 interface, where you visually design and build apps for Android devices, is online at **ai2.appinventor.mit.edu** App Inventor requires you to sign in with a Google account.

 Open a web browser and navigate to **accounts.google.com** then complete the form there to create a Google account

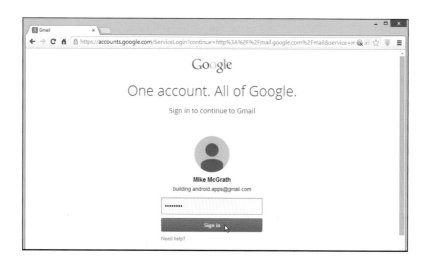

Next, attempt to navigate to the App Inventor 2 interface at **ai2.appinventor.mit.edu** – you will be redirected to a Google Sign In page

Now, enter your Google account details to sign in

Hot tip

Use your existing Google account to sign in if you already have one.

...cont'd

After signing in you will be redirected to the App Inventor 2 interface. Upon your first visit, App Inventor opens in "Projects mode" with no previously created projects and looks like this:

App Inventor 2 runs entirely in the web browser – unlike the previous version that required Java support.

④ Click the "New Project" button to launch the New App Inventor Project dialog

⑤ Type the Project Name **Hello** and click OK – to see a new empty project appear

Name new projects capitalized with an uppercase first character.

Exploring the designer

Having created an App Inventor project, as described on the previous page, it can be opened for work in "Designer mode".

 On the App Inventor Projects page click on the project item you wish to open – see App Inventor switch to its Designer mode with the chosen project opened

New Project	Delete Project

Projects

	Name	Date Created
☑	**Hello**	2014 May 4 11:33:55

2 Examine the green App Inventor title bar to see it contains the app name, buttons to work on multi-screen apps, and buttons to switch between Designer mode and a "Blocks" editor mode

3 Now, explore the App Inventor Designer to see it comprises these five columns:

The Media column is located directly below the Components column.

● **Palette:** containing individual components that can be added to the interface, grouped by category – such as "User Interface"

● **Viewer:** visually representing components added to the interface – a screen container component is provided by default

● **Components:** listing components added to the interface – arranged hierarchically beneath the screen component

● **Media:** listing media resources used by the app – such as images, audio, and video files

● **Properties:** listing editable characteristics of the component currently selected in the Viewer column – such as "Screen1"

4 Finally, notice that the top App Inventor menu bar remains constant in any view – click the "My Projects" menu item at any time to return to the Projects page

You can also return to the Projects page at any time by choosing the "My Projects" item on the "Projects" menu.

13

Adding components

The first stage in creating an app is to design the user interface by adding components from the Palette column in Designer mode. Follow these easy steps to add components to the Hello project, begun on the previous page, on your own system:

 Click on the Palette column's User Interface category to reveal the component items it contains

 Next, click on a Label component in the Palette column's User Interface category and drag a copy of it to the Viewer column – release the mouse button to drop it

Hot tip

Notice that when a component gets dropped onto the Viewer it gets added to the list of items in the Components column and its characteristics appear in the Properties column.

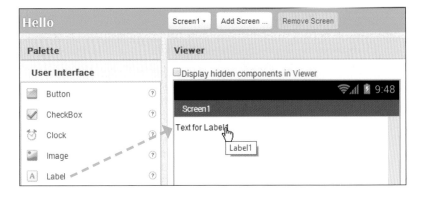

 Now, click on a Button component in the Palette column's User Interface category and drag a copy of it to the Viewer column – release the mouse button to drop it

Hot tip

At any time in Designer mode you can click on a component in the Viewer to "select" it and see it get highlighted in the Components column, and then see its characteristics appear in the Properties column.

14

4 Click on the Label component added to the Viewer to select it – see its characteristics appear in the Properties column

Items listed in the Properties column can be edited by clicking on them to change text values, check/uncheck boxes, or choose from alternatives that appear in pop-up dialog boxes.

5 Edit the Label component's characteristics in the Properties column to set its BackgroundColor to "Blue", FontBold to checked, FontSize to "30", Text to blank, TextColor to "Yellow", Width to "Fill parent", and Height to "40" – see the Label's look change in the Viewer

6 Now, click on the Button component in the Viewer to select it – see its characteristics appear in the Properties column

7 Edit the Button component's characteristics in the Properties column to set its FontSize to "30" and Text to "Click Me" – see the Button's look change in the Viewer

Properties

Label1

BackgroundColor
■ Blue

FontBold
☑

FontItalic
☐

FontSize
30.0

FontTypeface
default ▼

Text
[   ]

TextAlignment
left ▼

TextColor
☐ Yellow

Visible
showing ▼

Width
Fill parent...

Height
40 pixels...

The components added to the Viewer have been automatically named "Label1" and "Button1" by App Inventor but as yet have no functionality. The next stage in creating an app is to add functionality – making the Button respond to a user action by displaying a response message in the Label component.

Applying behaviors

The second stage in creating an app is to apply functionality to components added to the user interface in App Inventor Designer. This stage employs the App Inventor "Blocks mode" editor that allows you to easily add functionality without writing any program code. Follow these easy steps to add "Click" behavior functionality to components of the Hello project, added on the previous page:

1 On the App Inventor menu bar, click on the "Blocks" button – to switch to the Blocks mode editor

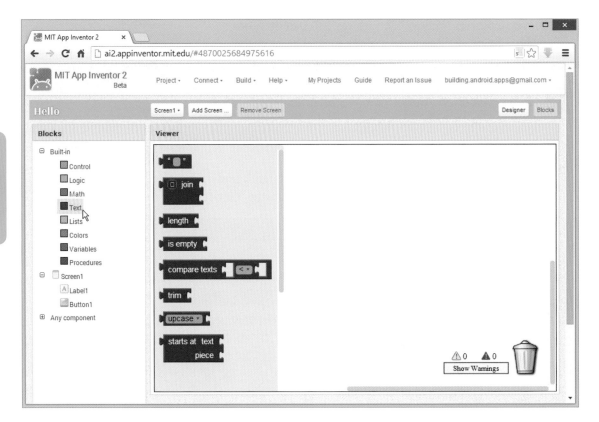

The Blocks mode editor has a "Blocks" column listing "drawers" (nodes) that each provide various individual colored blocks of code text that can be snapped together, like jigsaw-puzzle pieces, to form instructions to be performed by the app. The selection of blocks available for any listed drawer appear when you click on that drawer in the Blocks column. The blocks are assembled by choosing an available block then dragging it onto the Blocks editor's "Viewer" area.

2 Click on the **Button1** drawer – to reveal its blocks

3 Now, drag the top block containing the text **when Button1.Click do** onto the Blocks editor's Viewer area

Hello	Screen1 ▾	Add Screen ...	Remove Screen

Blocks | **Viewer**

- ⊕ Built-in
- ⊖ ☐ Screen1
  - A Label1
  - Button1
- ⊕ Any component

when Button1 .Click
do

App Inventor 2 automatically adds a corresponding component drawer directly in the editor's Blocks column whenever you add a component in Designer mode – unlike the previous version that placed them into a "My Blocks" drawer.

4 Click the **Label1** drawer and drag the **set Label1.Text to** block to the Viewer – snapping it into the previous block

Hello	Screen1 ▾	Add Screen ...	Remove Screen

Blocks | **Viewer**

- ⊕ Built-in
- ⊖ ☐ Screen1
  - A Label1
  - Button1
- ⊕ Any component

when Button1 ▾ .Click
do set Label1 ▾ . Text ▾ to

17

5 Click the Built-in **Text** drawer and drag its " " basic text block onto the Viewer and snap it into the previous block

6 Finally, click on the text block's " " content area, to make it editable, and change the content to **"Hello World!"**

Hello	Screen1 ▾	Add Screen ...	Remove Screen

Blocks | **Viewer**

- ⊖ Built-in
  - ☐ Control
  - ☐ Logic
  - ☐ Math
  - ☐ Text
  - ☐ Lists

when Button1 ▾ .Click
do set Label1 ▾ . Text ▾ to " Hello World! "

If you snap together blocks that form an invalid instruction, the Blocks editor will advise you of the error.

Running your first app

The recommended way to build apps with App Inventor requires your computer to share a WiFi connection with your Android device, so you can run the app as you build it for "live testing", and the **MIT AI2 Companion** to be installed on the Android device to allow a "handshake" connection to be established between App Inventor and the device using a generated code.

1 On your Android device, go the Google Play Store and install the MIT AI2 Companion

 Google play

Installation of the MIT AI2 Companion is best done from the Play store. Loading the Companion directly ("side loading") means it will not receive automatic updates.

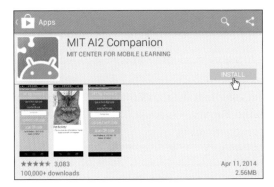

2 On your computer, with the Hello app open in App Inventor, choose Connect > AI Companion on the menu to see a generated 6-character code

The option shown to connect via USB is fraught with driver issues so is best avoided.

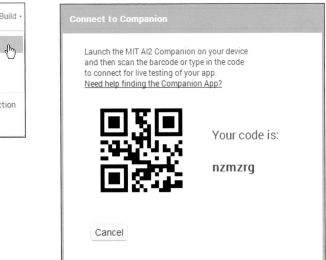

Connect to Companion

Launch the MIT AI2 Companion on your device and then scan the barcode or type in the code to connect for live testing of your app.
Need help finding the Companion App?

Your code is:

nzmzrg

3 Back on your Android device, launch the MIT AI2 Companion and see it request you type in a handshake code

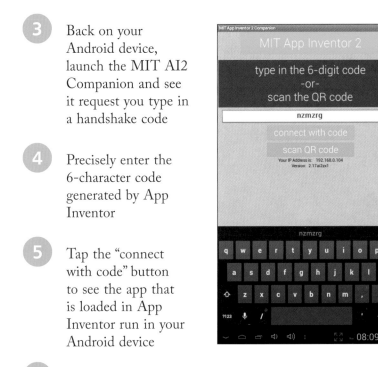

4 Precisely enter the 6-character code generated by App Inventor

The computer running App Inventor in a browser must be connected to the same WiFi network as the Android device running the MIT AI2 Companion.

5 Tap the "connect with code" button to see the app that is loaded in App Inventor run in your Android device

6 Tap the Button component in the Hello app running on the Android device to see the behavior defined in the Blocks editor apply the Label text greeting message

The running app can be updated live – try changing the label color in App Inventor's Designer mode to see it immediately change in the Android device.

Testing by emulator

As an alternative to live testing apps with an actual Android device, an Android device emulator can be used on your computer. This requires that **aiStarter** be installed on your computer from **appinventor.mit.edu/explore/ai2/setup-emulator.html**
Once installed, the aiStarter program typically starts automatically when you start your computer, or it can be started manually.

1 Ensure the aiStarter program is running – on Windows you will see a command window appear like this one

aiStarter

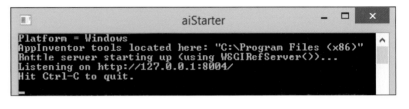

2 With the Hello app open in App Inventor choose Connect > Emulator on the menu to see the emulator app start up followed by an AI Companion app start up

Don't forget

The AI Companion app here gets automatically installed when the aiStarter gets installed on the computer.

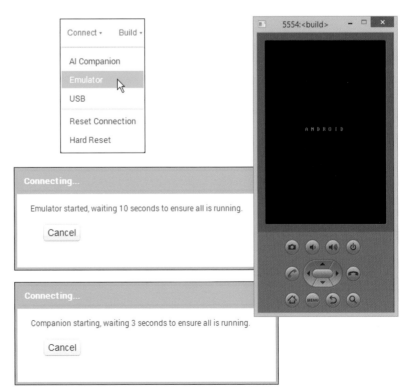

3 Wait until the initial black screen of the emulator changes to color, then wait until the emulator's SD card loads

4 Continue to wait while the AI Companion loads the Hello app from App Inventor

Starting the emulator can take a couple of minutes but you should simply wait until your app appears in the emulator screen – don't use the emulator before.

5 Click the Button component in the Hello app running on the emulator to see the behavior defined in the Blocks editor apply the Label text greeting message

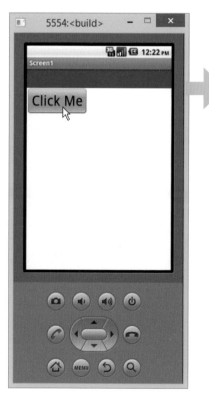

Help for trouble shooting connection problems can be found online at **appinventor.mit.edu/ explore/ai2/ connection-help.html**

Installing your first app

When you have completed building an app in App Inventor it can be compiled into an APK Android package and downloaded for direct installation ("side loaded") onto any Android device.

Hello.apk

 With the Hello app open in App Inventor choose the Build > "App (save .apk to my computer)" menu option

Build ▾	Help ▾
App (provide QR code for .apk)	
App (save .apk to my computer)	

2 Wait while App Inventor compiles the project then downloads the APK package to your computer

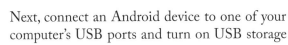

Progress Bar for Hello

95%

Building APK

3 Next, connect an Android device to one of your computer's USB ports and turn on USB storage

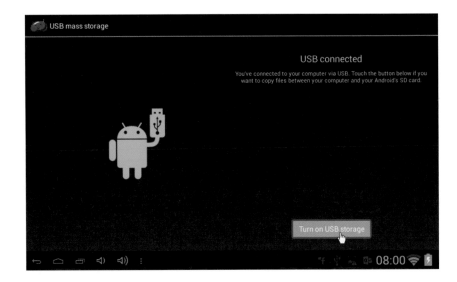

4 Now, copy the APK package from the default download folder on your computer to a convenient folder on the connected Android device

5 Ensure that the Settings on the Android device allow "installation of apps from unknown sources"

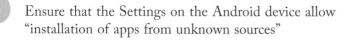

23

6 Tap the Hello.apk package icon on the Android device to call up the Android installer, then tap Install

7 When installation completes, tap Open to launch the application or tap the Hello icon that has been added

Managing projects

The "Projects" menu on the App Inventor menu bar contains a number of useful options for managing your application projects. Whenever you make any change to an app you are developing, App Inventor automatically saves the project, ensuring it is constantly up-to-date – so the "Save project" option is seldom needed. Its "Save project as" option is useful to create a new copy of the project, and you then continue working on that new copy. Its "Checkpoint" option, on the other hand, is useful to create a new backup copy of the project, and you then continue working on the original project:

Automatic saving also enables changes to be instantly implemented during live testing.

1. With the Hello project open, click on the Project > Checkpoint option and accept the suggested default name to create a backup of this project

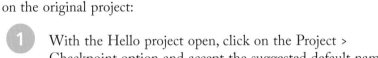

As you develop more applications with App Inventor each project gets automatically saved in the list on the "My Projects" page. While in App Inventor's Projects mode, projects can be added to the list at any time using the "New Project" button or "Start new project" option, and existing projects can be deleted using the "Delete Project" button or "Delete project" option:

The New Project and Delete Project buttons are only accessible on the My Projects page, but the Start new project and Delete project options are accessible on the Projects menu while in Designer mode or Blocks editor mode.

2. In the My Projects list, check the box against the Hello project backup then click the Delete Project button or choose the Projects > "Delete project" option to remove it

Besides sharing your apps with others in an executable form as an Android package (.apk) for installation on an Android device, you can share your apps in source code form as an App Inventor Archive (.aia) that can be loaded into App Inventor and remixed.

3 In the My Projects list, check the box against the Hello project then choose the Projects > "Export project (.aia) to my computer" option to download the project source code

App Inventor 2 compresses resources into a single AIA archive – unlike the previous version that compressed them into a ZIP archive. Both archive types can be explored with a file archiver such as the free 7-Zip tool from **7-zip.org**

4 Delete the Hello project from the My Projects list using either of the methods described in Step 2

5 Click Projects > "Import project (.aia) from my computer" then choose the downloaded AIA source file to restore the project to the My Projects list

The AIA sources of each example in this book are contained in the free ZIP archive described on page 6, so you can upload and remix them.

Summary

- Android is an operating system for mobile phones and tablets

- App Inventor enables you to develop applications for Android devices without writing a single line of code

- MIT App Inventor 2 runs completely in a web browser

- App Inventor first opens on the Projects page where new projects get started

- The App Inventor Designer mode is where you add components to the application to design the user interface

- Designer mode contains Palette, Viewer, Components, Media, and Properties columns

- Interface components can be dragged from the Palette onto the Viewer and their characteristics edited in Properties

- The App Inventor Blocks editor mode is where you add functionality to the application to create behaviors

- Blocks editor mode contains a Blocks column, listing drawers that each provide blocks of code, and a Viewer area

- Blocks can be dragged from the Blocks column and snapped together on the Viewer area to form instructions

- MIT AI2 Companion enables an Android device to be used for live testing an app via a shared WiFi network connection

- Installation of aiStarter enables a virtual device emulator to be used to test an app on a single computer

- Completed apps can be compiled as an APK package for download and then be side loaded onto Android devices

- Project source code can be downloaded as an AIA archive for sharing and be uploaded for remixing

- Projects are managed from the My Projects list view

2 Designing interfaces

This chapter demonstrates how to use components of the App Inventor User Interface palette for interface design in Android apps.

Enabling buttons

A Button component provides an easy way for the user to interact with an Android application. Tapping a button in the interface creates a "Click event" within the app. The application may then respond by calling a Click "event-handler" behavior to perform a task, such as write a response message on a Label component.

Optionally, a Button's properties may be changed as the application proceeds to reflect its current status. For example, its "Enabled" property can be toggled on or off – to make the Button active or inactive according to the app requirements:

Button.apk

 Start a new App Inventor project named "Button" then set the screen's Title property to "Button"

 From the User Interface palette, drag a Label component and two Button components onto the Viewer

3 In the Components column, rename the components **lblMessage**, **btnStart** and **btnStop** respectively

4 In the Properties column, edit the components' BackgroundColor, TextColor, FontSize, and Text properties so they resemble the screenshot below:

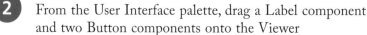

5 Next, in the Properties column, uncheck the **btnStop** component's Enabled property to change its default state – so it will not be active when the application launches

 Launch the Blocks editor – ready to add event-handler behaviors for each Button's Click event

7 Click the button component drawers in turn and drag **btnStop.Click** and **btnStart.Click** blocks onto the Viewer

8 Snap **set lblMessage.Text**, **set btnStart.Enabled**, and **set btnStop.Enabled** blocks into both of the Button's **.Click** blocks on the Viewer

9 Now snap " " basic text blocks into the **set lblMessage. Text** blocks and edit their content to assign appropriate Label text values – reflecting a running or stopped state

Each component item has blocks to **set** and **get** its property values.

10 From the Built-in Logic drawer, snap **true** and **false** Boolean value blocks into the **set btnStart.Enabled**, and **set btnStop.Enabled** blocks to toggle their active status

11 Run the application in the emulator or a device, then tap the buttons to see them perform their attached behaviors – changing the Label text and toggling the Button states

Some blocks, such as the **set** blocks and logic blocks shown here, now have a clickable ▾ "dropdown" button that allow you to quickly modify the block by choosing components, properties, or values.

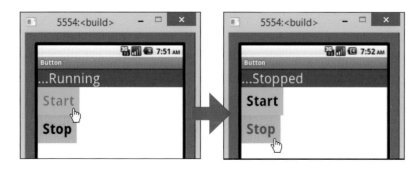

29

Reading text input

A TextBox component is an essential part of many Android applications, allowing the user to input text for use by the app, where content typed in the TextBox is readable on the screen.

A PasswordTextBox component allows the user to input sensitive text for use by the app, such as a passwords, where content typed in the PasswordTextBox is not readable on the screen.

TextBox.apk

 Start a new App Inventor project named "TextBox" then set the screen's Title property to "TextBox"

 From the User Interface palette, drag a Label, a TextBox, a PasswordTextBox, and a Button onto the Viewer

3 In the Components column, rename the components **lblMessage**, **txtUserName**, **txtPassword** and **btnApply**

4 In the Properties column, edit the components' properties so they resemble the screenshot below:

> 📶 🔋 9:48
>
> TextBox
>
> **...ready**
>
> ```
> ••••••••••
> ```
>
> Apply Input

 Launch the Blocks editor – ready to add an event-handler to read user input when the Button gets clicked

 From the button's drawer drag a **btnApply.Click** block onto the Viewer

7 Snap **set lblMessage.Text**, **set txtUserName.Text** and **set txtPassword.Text** blocks into the Button's **.Click** block on the Viewer

Hot tip

With a TextBox component selected on the Viewer you can add its input hint for the user as the Hint item in the Property column.

...cont'd

8 From the Built-in Text drawer, snap " " basic text blocks into the **set txtUserName.Text** and **set txtPassword.Text** blocks – to assign empty text to each TextBox when the Button gets clicked

9 Next, from the Built-in Text drawer, snap a single **join** block into the **set lblMessage.Text** block – providing empty sockets for two text blocks to be added

Hot tip

Click on a text block's content to make it active then hit the Delete key on your keyboard to remove the content.

10 Now, snap **txtUserName.Text** and **txtPassword.Text** blocks into the **join** block – to assign a concatenated (joined) text string to the Label when the Button gets clicked

11 Run the application then enter text in the boxes and click the Button to read your text input into the Label

Don't forget

With the Label's Height property set to Automatic, its height automatically increases to accommodate the applied text string.

31

Inserting images

An Image component allows images and photos to be displayed in your application. The properties of the Image component specify the actual image file to be displayed and aspects of its appearance, such as width and height.

Supported image file formats are JPG, PNG, GIF, and BMP.

An image is added to an application using the Image component's Picture property. Its Upload File button can directly specify an image file to be uploaded for inclusion in the app, or select an image file that has been already uploaded as a Media resource.

Image.apk

 1 Start a new App Inventor project named "Image" then set the screen's Title property to "Image"

 2 From the User Interface palette, drag two Image components onto the Viewer

 3 In the Components column, rename the components **imgRed** and **imgBlue**

4 Select the **imgRed** component, then click its Picture item in the Properties column and click the Upload File button that appears – to launch the Upload File dialog box

5 In the Upload File dialog box, click the Choose File button and choose an image for upload, then click OK to see that image appear in the component on the Viewer

Hot tip

The file name of uploaded image files gets automatically added to the list of application resources that appears in the Media column.

Properties
imgRed
Picture
redAndroid.png...

 6 In the Media column, click the Upload File button to launch the Upload File dialog box

7 In the Upload File dialog box, click the Choose File button and choose an image for upload, then click OK to see its file name get added to the Media resources list

 8 Select the **imgBlue** component, then click its Picture item in the Properties column and choose an image resource from the dropdown list that appears

 9 Click OK to see your chosen image appear in the component on the Viewer

The PNG and GIF image file formats both support alpha transparency – so you can have transparent image backgrounds.

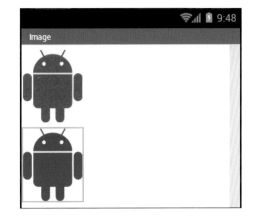

 **10** Run the application in the emulator or in a connected device to see the images appear on the screen

By default, an Image component's Visible property is enabled, but can be disabled by unchecking that item in the Properties column – ensure it is enabled to see the image appear.

Painting canvas

A Canvas component provides a powerful touch-sensitive rectangular area on the screen in which the application can draw shapes and text, and allow user interaction with touch and drag.

Shapes can be drawn on a Canvas by the application when the app first launches using the screen's Initialize event-handler block.

Canvas.apk

 Start a new App Inventor project named "Canvas" then set the screen's Title property to "Canvas"

 From the Drawing and Animation palette, drag a Canvas component onto the Viewer

3 In the Components column, rename the component **canBullseye**

4 In the Properties column, set both the Width and Height to 200 pixels, and set the BackgroundColor to Blue – to specify the component's appearance

Canvas

📶 🔋 9:48

Hot tip

Further examples of the versatile Canvas component, showing its use for animation and games, are provided in following chapters.

 Now, in the Properties column, set the PaintColor to Red – to specify the brush color with which to begin drawing

6 Launch the Blocks editor – ready to add an event-handler to draw on the Canvas when the app initializes

 Drag a **Screen1.Initialize** block onto the Viewer from the Screen's drawer

8 Next, drag a **call canBullseye.DrawCircle** block from the Canvas's drawer and snap it into the **Initialize** block

9 Snap Math number blocks into each of the three sockets of the **canBullseye.DrawCircle** block – to draw a circle of 100 pixels radius, centered at X:100, Y:100 on the Canvas

Hot tip

Click on the Viewer and type **100** to create a number block with a value of 100, or drag one from the Built-In tab's Math item.

10 Now, snap a **set canBullseye.PaintColor** block into the **Initialize** block (below the **DrawCircle** block) and snap a yellow Colors block into its socket to change brush color

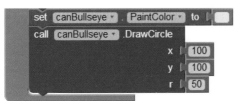

11 Snap a second **call canBullseye.DrawCircle** block into the **Initialize** block (below the **PaintColor** block) and snap number values of 100, 100, and 50 into its sockets – to draw a circle of 50 pixels radius, centered on the Canvas

12 Run the application in the emulator or a connected device to see the Canvas appear with the specified appearance and see colored circles drawn at the specified coordinates

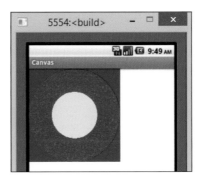

Hot tip

Click on the Viewer and type **yellow** to create a yellow color block, or drag one from the Built-in Colors drawer.

Picking list items

A ListPicker component provides the user with an easy way to select an item from a list of text options in an Android application. Tapping a ListPicker in the interface reveals the list of options to the user and an AfterPicking event occurs when an item gets selected. The application may then respond by calling an AfterPicking "event-handler" to perform a task, such as write the selection on a Label component.

ListPicker.apk

 1 Start a new App Inventor project named "ListPicker" then set the screen's Title property to "ListPicker"

2 From the User Interface palette, drag a Label component and a ListPicker component onto the Viewer

3 In the Components column, rename the components **lblMessage**, and **lprColors** respectively

4 In the Properties column, edit the components' BackgroundColor, FontSize, and Text properties so they resemble the screenshot below:

ListPicker

Select an item

The appearance of a ListPicker component initially resembles a Button component on the screen, but will switch to a list view when it gets tapped.

5 Select the ListPicker component, then in the Properties column type a comma-separated list of colors into the ElementsFromString field – to specify a list of options

ElementsFromString

Red,Green,Blue

6 Launch the Blocks editor – ready to add an event-handler behavior for the AfterPicking event

7 From the ListPicker's drawer drag a **when lprColors.AfterPicking** block onto the Viewer

8 Snap a **set lblMessage.Text** block into the empty socket of the **AfterPicking** block

9 Now, snap a **lprColors.Selection** block into the **Text** block – to assign the selected text value to the Label

10 Run the application in the emulator or a connected device then choose an option from the available list to see your selection appear on the Label

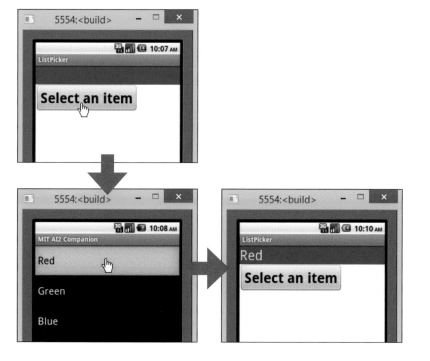

Do not confuse the **ListPicker.Selection** block, which contains selected option text value, with the **ListPicker.Text** block, which contains the button face text value.

Examples demonstrating how to create option lists in the Blocks editor are provided in following chapters.

Checking boxes

A Checkbox component allows the user to optionally select individual items in an Android application by checking a box. The Text value of the Checkbox can be processed by the app.

When a CheckBox has been checked its state is set to **true**, otherwise its state is **false**. The action of checking a CheckBox therefore changes its state and so fires a Changed event. The application may then respond by calling a Changed "event-handler" to perform a task, such as write the CheckBox's associated Text value on a Label component.

CheckBox.apk

 Start a new App Inventor project named "CheckBox" then set the screen's Title property to "CheckBox"

2 From the User Interface palette, drag a Label component and a CheckBox component onto the Viewer

3 In the Components column, rename the components **lblMessage** and **chkItem**

4 In the Properties column, edit the components' properties so they resemble the screenshot below:

Whatever you type into a CheckBox's Text field in the Properties column appears alongside the component in the interface and is also its associated Text value.

5 Launch the Blocks editor – ready to add an event-handler to write the CheckBox's associated Text and its current state on the Label whenever it gets changed

6 Drag a **when chkItem.Changed** block onto the Viewer and snap a **set lblMessage.Text** block into its socket

7 Snap a **chkItem.Text** block into a **join** Text block then snap them both into the **set lblMessage.Text** block

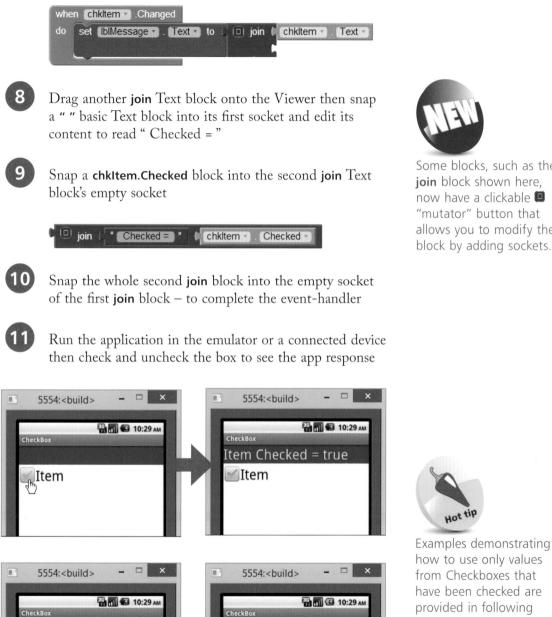

8 Drag another **join** Text block onto the Viewer then snap a " " basic Text block into its first socket and edit its content to read " Checked = "

9 Snap a **chkItem.Checked** block into the second **join** Text block's empty socket

Some blocks, such as the **join** block shown here, now have a clickable ▣ "mutator" button that allows you to modify the block by adding sockets.

10 Snap the whole second **join** block into the empty socket of the first **join** block – to complete the event-handler

11 Run the application in the emulator or a connected device then check and uncheck the box to see the app response

Examples demonstrating how to use only values from Checkboxes that have been checked are provided in following chapters.

Storing data

A TinyDB component is a non-visible component that provides an easy way to dynamically store and retrieve data in an Android application. The data must be assigned a tag name of your choice when it gets stored, then can be recalled using your chosen name. TinyDB is a persistent data store for the app – so the data stored there will be available each time the app is run. For example, a game's high score can be retrieved each time the game is played.

TinyDB.apk

1 Start a new App Inventor project named "TinyDB" then set the screen's Title property to "TinyDB"

2 Drag a Label, a TextBox, and two Buttons onto the Viewer, then add a TinyDB component from the Storage palette

3 In the Components column, rename the components **lblMessage**, **txtInput**, **btnSave** and **btnRestore** respectively

4 In the Properties column, edit the visible components' properties so they resemble the screenshot below:

> 9:48
>
> **TinyDB**
>
> **Save**
> **Restore**

When you drop a TinyDB component onto the Viewer it gets added to the Non-Visible Components list – below the Viewer's screen area.

5 Launch the Blocks editor and drag a **when btnSave.Click** block onto the Viewer, then snap a **call TinyDB1.StoreValue** block inside it

6 Add a " " basic Text block with a name of your choice to the **StoreValue** block's **tag** socket and a **txtInput.Text** block to its **valueToStore** socket – to assign current text to a tag

7 Add a **set txtInput.Text** block with an empty " " basic Text block – to clear all current text from the TextBox

8 Drag a **when btnRestore.Click** block onto the Viewer, then snap a **set lblMessage.Text** block inside it

9 Add a **call TinyDB1.GetValue** block with a " " basic Text block specifying the tag name of the stored data item – to display its content on the Label

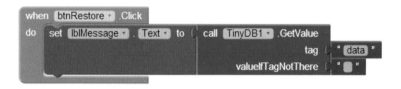

Hot tip

Assigning an empty " " text block to a TextBox component simply clears any existing content from that text field.

10 Run the application then enter some data into the text field, and use the buttons to save and restore its content

Beware

Data stored in a TinyDB is persistent only when the app has been installed on a device.

Telling the time

A Clock component is a non-visible component that fires a Timer event at a regular interval in an Android application. The Timer event is typically set to an interval of 1000 milliseconds (1 second) so could be used to update the seconds counter of a clock display.

Timers can be stopped and started by disabling/enabling their Clock component – to imitate the action of a stopwatch counter.

Clock.apk

 Start a new App Inventor project named "Clock" then set the screen's Title property to "Clock"

 From the User Interface palette, drag a Label component, a Clock component, and two Buttons onto the Viewer

3 In the Components column, rename the components **lblMessage**, **btnStart**, and **btnStop** respectively

4 In the Properties column, edit the visible components' properties so they resemble the screenshot below:

Properties

Clock1

TimerAlwaysFires
☑

TimerEnabled
☑

TimerInterval
1000

	📶 🔋 9:48
Clock	
0	
Start	
Stop	

5 Select the Clock component and set its Properties to be enabled and always fire at an interval of 1000 milliseconds

6 Launch the Blocks editor and drag a **when Clock1.Timer** block onto the Viewer

7 Snap a **set lblMessage.Text** block into the **.Timer** block then add a Math arithmetic + block

8 Snap a **lblMessage.Text** and Math number **1** block into the + block – to increment the value when the timer fires

...cont'd

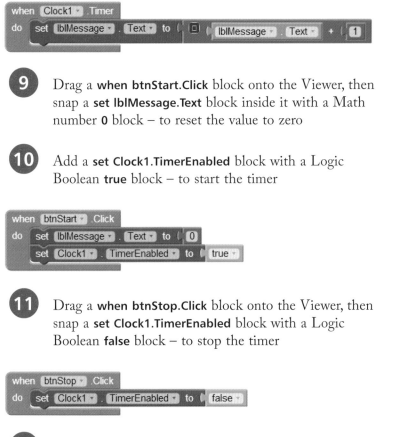

9 Drag a **when btnStart.Click** block onto the Viewer, then snap a **set lblMessage.Text** block inside it with a Math number **0** block – to reset the value to zero

10 Add a **set Clock1.TimerEnabled** block with a Logic Boolean **true** block – to start the timer

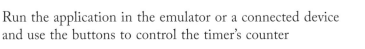

11 Drag a **when btnStop.Click** block onto the Viewer, then snap a **set Clock1.TimerEnabled** block with a Logic Boolean **false** block – to stop the timer

12 Run the application in the emulator or a connected device and use the buttons to control the timer's counter

Set this Label component's Text property to zero in its Properties column.

43

The Clock timer is a powerful, versatile component that is widely used for animation and game applications. Examples of these are provided in following chapters.

Configuring screens

Components added to the Viewer are, by default, arranged vertically – one above the other at the left edge of the screen. Interface layout can be better controlled using components from the Layout palette. This provides invisible containers that arrange the components they contain vertically, horizontally, or within cells of a table grid.

Arrangement.apk

 1 Start a new App Inventor project named "Arrangement" then set the screen's Title property to "Arrangement"

2 From the Layout palette, drag a HorizontalArrangement component onto the Viewer

3 Now, from the User Interface palette, drag a TextBox and a Button inside the HorizontalArrangement component – to see the container arrange them side-by-side

🛜📶🔋 9:48	
Arrangement	
[ ]	Text for Button1

4 Next, from the Layout palette, drag a TableArrangement component onto the Viewer – by default this will typically have a 2x2 grid of cells

5 From the User Interface palette, drag Buttons inside each cell of the TableArrangement component – to see the container arrange them in a grid layout

🛜📶🔋 9:48	
Arrangement	
[ ]	Text for Button1
Text for Button2	Text for Button3
Text for Button4	Text for Button5

Don't forget

You can adjust the number of table rows and columns in the TableArrangement component's Properties column.

Screen content can also be centered by clever use of the Layout Arrangement components and "padding" by Label components.

6 From the Layout palette, drag a HorizontalArrangement component onto the Viewer and drag a VerticalArrangement component inside it

7 Now, from the User Interface palette, drag two Labels into the HorizontalArrangement component – dropping one on each side of the VerticalArrangement component

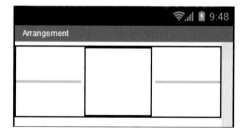

As you drag components onto Layout Arrangement containers a marker appears in the Viewer to indicate how they will be arranged.

8 Select the HorizontalArrangement component then in the Properties column change its Width to "Fill parent..." – to see it expand to fit the available screen width

9 Now, with each Label component, delete the default content from their Text property and also set their Width property to "Fill parent..." – to see them expand to center the VerticalArrangement component on the screen

Further components placed within this VerticalArrangement component will now appear centered on the screen:

This centering technique requires that the Width property of the Labels' parent container (i.e. the HorizontalArrangement) must be "Fill parent".

Summary

- Tapping a Button in the interface creates a Click event to which the app may respond using an event-handler

- A Button's Enabled property can be toggled on or off to make the Button active or inactive as required by the app

- TextBox and PasswordTextBox components both allow the user to input text for use by the app

- An Image component allows images and photos to be used in the app by specifying the name of an image file to display

- Images can be added using the Image component's Property column, or the Upload File button in the Media column

- A Canvas component provides a rectangular area on the screen in which the app can draw shapes and text

- Shapes can be drawn on a Canvas when the app launches using the screen's Initialize event-handler

- Selecting an option from a ListPicker creates an AfterPicking event to which the app may respond using an event-handler

- Checking a CheckBox creates a Changed event to which the app may respond using an event-handler

- A TinyDB component allows the app to dynamically store and retrieve data using an assigned tag name of your choice

- Data stored in a TinyDB is persistent so will be available each time the app is run

- A Clock component fires an event at a regular interval to which the app may respond using an event-handler

- Timers can be stopped and started by disabling and enabling their Clock component

- Interface layout can be better controlled using Arrangement components from the Layout palette

3 Controlling progress

This chapter demonstrates the mechanics of programming structures that allow data to be stored, controlled, and manipulated to progress an Android app.

Composing programs

An application is simply a series of program instructions that tell the device what to do. Although programs can be complex, each instruction is generally simple. The device starts at the beginning and works through, instruction by instruction, until it gets to the end. Here are the essential elements of Android app programs:

Statements
A statement is an instruction that performs a program task. For example, the statement **set Label1.Text to "Hello World!"** sets the text on the **Label1** component to the specified string value.

Procedures
A procedure is a group of one or more statements that may be called upon at any time for execution by the program. For example, the statement **call writeLabels** calls upon a procedure to execute statements that might assign values to Label components.

Variables
A variable is a named container defined in the program that stores a value. For example, the statement **initialize global Message to "Hello World!"** stores the string value in a variable called **Message**.

Operators
An operator performs a particular operation, such as **+** addition, **-** subtraction, **x** multiplication, and **/** division arithmetic operators.

Objects
An object is a program's fundamental "building block" entity. It can be visible, like a Button, or invisible like a Timer component.

Properties
A property is a characteristic of an object. For example, the property **Label1.Text** is the **Text** property of the **Label1** object.

Methods
A method is an action that an object can perform. For example, the method **Button1.Click** is the **Click** method of the **Button1** object.

Comments
A comment is a note describing the purpose of a statement. For example, "Clear the list" might describe a call to a **Clear** procedure.

The examples in this chapter demonstrate the various elements of a program. Refer back here for identification.

The App Inventor IDE is a safe environment in which to experiment and learn from your mistakes.

The illustration below shows the Blocks editor view of App Inventor programming code for the Click event-handler of a Button component.

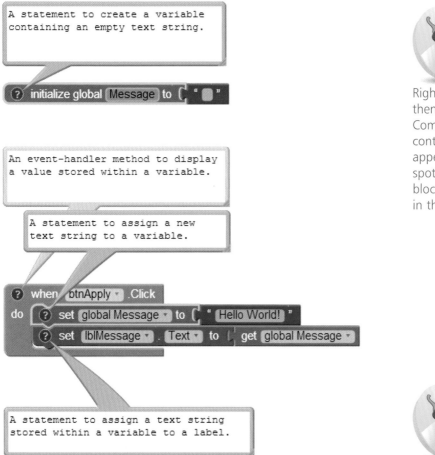

Blocks in App Inventor are colored to indicate particular parts of the program – to differentiate event-handler methods, procedures, variables, numeric values, text values, Boolean values (true/false), control routines, and list methods.

Defining variables

In Android App programming a "variable" is simply a useful container in which a value may be stored for subsequent use. The stored value may be changed (vary) as the program executes its instructions – hence the term "variable".

A variable is created in the App Inventor Blocks editor by first dragging an **initialize global** block from the Built-in Variables drawer onto the Viewer. The variable must then be given a name by editing the block's default name. The given name should indicate the nature of its contents and must be unique within that program – duplicated names are strictly not allowed. Once named, the variable can then be assigned an initial value of any data type – text, number, or Boolean (true or false).

Beware

Variable names must be unique so the program knows to which value an instruction is referring.

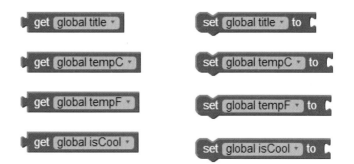

For each defined variable its given name gets automatically added to the dropdown list of the **get** and **set** Variables blocks that can be used to retrieve or assign that variable's stored value:

Hot tip

You can rename a variable at any time while building an app and its name on any associated blocks will be automatically updated.

The descriptions on the faces of the new blocks contain the term "global" to indicate that the variable is accessible globally within the program – any part of the program can get or set its value.

1 Start a new App Inventor project named "Variable" then add a Label component and a Button component

2 Launch the Blocks Editor then drag an **initialize global** block from the Variables drawer onto the Viewer area

3 Edit the default name on the **initialize global** block then add a Text block to set an initial value

4 Add an event-handler block for the screen's Intialize event that assigns the variable value to the Label

5 Now, add an event-handler block for the button's Click event that assigns a new text value to the variable value, then assigns that new variable value to the Label

6 Finally, run the app to see the initial variable value appear on the Label upon launch, then click the Button to see the new variable value appear on the Label

Variable.apk

Hot tip

You can also create "local" variables within procedure blocks of code – an example featuring a local variable is provided on page 76.

51

Don't forget

Simply click on the name in a block to set it active so it can be edited.

Performing operations

Operators in the Built-in Math drawer allow an Android App to progress by performing arithmetical tasks with two given numerical values (operands), or by comparing two given operands.

Arithmetical operators

The arithmetical operators **+**, **-**, **x**, and **/** (divide) return the result of an operation performed on two given operands, and act as you would expect. For example, the expression **5 + 2** returns **7**.

Additionally, the **modulo** function divides the first operand by the second operand and returns the remainder of the operation. For example, the expression **32 modulo 5** returns 2 – five divides into thirty-two six times, with two remainder.

Care must be taken with complex expressions, which contain multiple arithmetical operators, to ensure that operations are performed in the required order to avoid undesirable results. Consider the expression **8 + 4 x 2**, for example. Performing operations in left-to-right order 8 + 4 = 12, then (**12**) x 2 = 24. But performing in right-to-left order 2 x 4 = 8, then (**8**) + 8 = **16**.

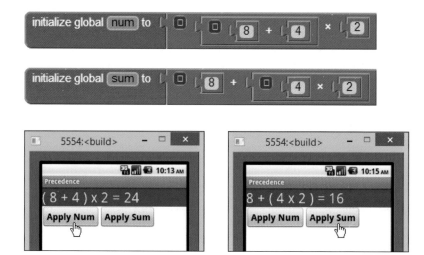

Don't forget

The **modulo** operator is useful to determine whether a given value is "odd" or "even".

Precedence.apk

...cont'd

Comparison operators

The comparison operators compare two given operands and return a single Boolean value of **true** or **false** – describing the result.

The **=** equality operator returns **true** when both operands <u>are</u> of equal value, otherwise it will return **false**. Conversely, the **≠** inequality operator returns **true** when both operands <u>are not</u> equal.

The **>** "greater-than" operator only returns **true** when the first operand is greater in value than the second operand, whereas the **<** "less-than" operator only returns **true** when the first operand is less in value than the second operator. Subtly different, the **≥** and **≤** operators work in a similar way but also return **true** when both operands are exactly equal.

Operators in the Built-in Logic drawer allow an Android App to progress by performing comparisons between "Boolean" operands. These are operands that are, or can convert to, **true** or **false** values.

The **and** operator will only return **true** when <u>both</u> operands are themselves **true**, whereas the **or** operator will only return **true** when <u>either one</u> of the operands are themselves **true**.

Usefully, the unary **not** operator returns the inverse Boolean state of the supplied operand – reversing **true** to **false**, and **false** to **true**.

Hot tip

The **=** equality and **not** **=** inequality operators are useful in testing the state of a variable to perform conditional branching – proceeding in particular directions according to the tested condition.

Hot tip

The **not** operator is useful to toggle the state of a variable in successive loop iterations – like flicking a light switch on and off with each pass.

53

Branching flow

The Built-in Control drawer contains a number of blocks that can be used to progress an Android App by making conditional tests. When a tested condition is **true** given statements get executed, otherwise the program moves on to subsequent statements. Conditional tests can also evaluate complex expressions to test multiple conditions for a **true** value using **and** and **or** Logic blocks.

If.apk

1 Start a new App Inventor project named "If" then add a Label, a TextBox, and a Button component

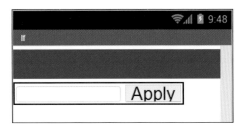

2 Launch the Blocks editor then drag in an event-handler for the button's Click event from the button's drawer

3 Add blocks to the event-handler – assigning default text to the Label when the Button gets clicked

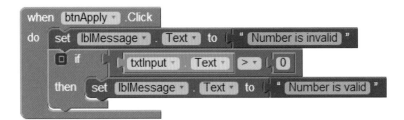

Don't forget

The default "invalid" text will appear in the Label unless the test is found to be true, so the new "valid" text gets inserted.

4 Drag an **if** block from the Built-in Control drawer, then add blocks to perform a conditional test – to determine whether the TextBox contains a positive numerical value

5 Add blocks to the **if** block – assigning new text to the Label when the test succeeds

6 Run the app then enter a positive number into the TextBox and click the Button to see the success message

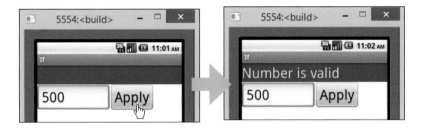

Hot tip

The range 1-1000 could also be tested with Math blocks specifying **≥ 1** (greater or equal to 1) and specifying **≤ 1000**. (less or equal to 1000).

7 Extend the conditional test by inserting an **and** block from the Logic drawer – to determine whether the TextBox contains a numerical value in the range 1-1000

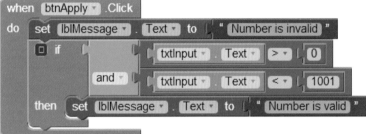

8 Further extend the conditional test by inserting an **or** block from the Logic drawer – to determine whether the TextBox contains a numerical value in the range 1-1000 or is exactly a value of 2000

Beware

This example attempts no validation so entering a non-numeric value will cause an error. The entry could first be tested, however, using the Math **is a number?** block.

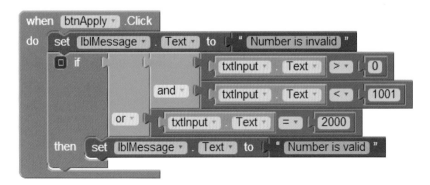

Providing alternatives

The **if** test block, described in the previous example, can be extended by clicking on the mutator button and adding an **else** socket to make an **if else** test block. This performs a conditional test, to seek a **true** condition, and also offers an alternative "branch" for the program to pursue when the condition is **false**. In its simplest form this merely nominates an alternative statement to execute when the test fails, but more powerful conditional tests can be constructed by "nesting" **if else** test blocks – one inside another. When the program finds a **true** condition it executes those associated statements then immediately exits the nested **if else** test blocks, without exploring any further branches.

IfElse.apk

1   Start a new App Inventor project named "IfElse" then add a Label component and a Button component

2   Launch the Blocks editor then drag an **initialize global** block from the Built-in Variables drawer and assign it a numeric value of 11

```
initialize global hours to  11
```

3   Drag in an event-handler for the button's Click event then snap in an **if** test block from the Control drawer and add an **else** socket – making an **if else** block

Conditional branching is the fundamental process by which all computer programs proceed.

4   Add blocks to the **if else** block's **if** socket to perform a conditional test – testing if the variable contains a numerical value below 13

5   Now, add blocks to the **if else** block's **then** socket – assigning new text to the Label when the test succeeds

6 Run the application then click the Button to see the text message appear as the test succeeds

7 Extend the conditional test by inserting a second **if else** block into the **else** socket of the first **if else** block

8 Now, add blocks to the second **if else** block's **if** socket to perform a conditional test – testing if the variable contains a numerical value below 18

9 Add blocks to the second **if else** block's sockets – assigning new text to the Label when the test succeeds, and assigning new text to the Label when the test fails

10 Adjust the value of the variable upwards, to say 15 or 20, then run the app and click the Button to see the appropriate text message appear

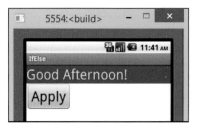

Notifying messages

The User Interface palette contains a Notifier component that provides pop-up "Alert" dialogs to the user in an Android App. Its drawer in the Blocks editor contains **ShowAlert** and **ShowMessageDialog** blocks to which text can be simply specified to determine what will be displayed on the dialog box they produce.

Two other dialogs can be provided to gain user input, by choosing from two button alternatives or by entering input into a TextBox.

Dialogs.apk

1. Start a new App Inventor project named "Dialogs" then add a Label, two Buttons, and two Notifier components – naming the Notifier components **dlgChoice** and **dlgInput**

2. Launch the Blocks editor then add a button Click event-handler and snap in a **call dlgChoice.ShowChooseDialog** block – adding text blocks for the dialog face and buttons

3. Add another button Click event-handler and from the **dlgInput** drawer snap in a **call dlgInput.ShowTextDialog** block – adding text blocks for the dialog face

Hot tip

The **ShowAlert** dialog simply displays a message but, unlike the **ShowMessage** dialog, it automatically disappears without requiring the click of an OK button.

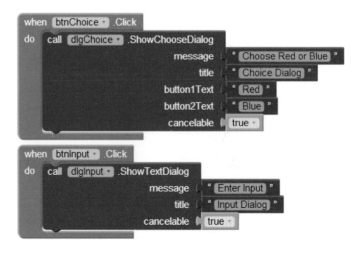

Next, add event-handlers to process the user's choice and input.

4 From the **dlgChoice** drawer, drag a **dlgChoice.AfterChoosing** block to the Viewer – a **choice** argument is provided that you can click to obtain a **get choice** block

Notice that the matching event-handler for the **ShowChooseDialog** is named **AfterChoosing** whereas the event-handler for the **ShowTextDialog** is named **AfterTextInput**.

5 Add a **set lblMessage.Text** block then snap in a **get choice** Variables block

6 From the **dlgInput** drawer drag a **dlgInput.AfterTextInput** block to the Viewer – a **response** block is provided that you can click to obtain a **get response** block

```
when  dlgInput ▼  .AfterTextInput
    response
do    set  lblMessage ▼  .  Text ▼  to    get  response ▼
```

7 Add a **set lblMessage.Text** block then snap in a **get response** block

8 Run the app then use the dialogs to get user input

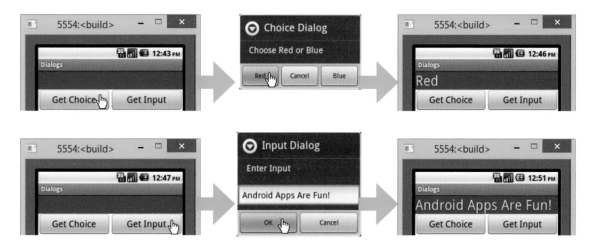

Looping within a range

Programming loop structures allow an Android App to progress by repeatedly executing specified statements, until the loop ends. Consequently, the specified statements must include a test expression to determine when to end – or they will run forever!

The popular **for each** loop uses a counter to test the number of times it has executed (iterated) its statements. This loop ends when it reaches the extreme of its specified range. It is often useful to incorporate the increasing value of the counter into the statements executed on each iteration of the loop.

ForRange.apk

1 Start a new App Inventor project named "ForRange" then add a Label component and a Button component – naming the components **lblMessage** and **btnApply**

2 Launch the Blocks editor, then add an event-handler for the button's Click event and snap in a **for each** block from the Built-in Control drawer – a loop argument named **number** is created automatically

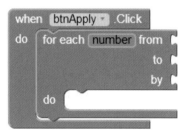

In programming, so-called "trivial" counter variables are typically named **i**, **j**, **k**.

3 Add a Math number **1** block to the **for each** block's **from** socket, a Math number **10** block to its **to** socket, and a Math number **1** block to its **by** socket – to specify the loop's range, making 10 iterations

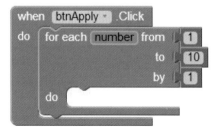

Next, add blocks stating what the loop should do on each iteration.

4 Drag in a **set lblMessage.Text** block and snap it into the **for each** block's **do** socket

5 From the Built-in Text drawer, add a **join** block to the **set lblMessage.Text** block – providing sockets to concatenate (join) values into a single text string

6 Snap blocks into the **join** block to assign a text string to the Label on each iteration, by dragging a **get number** block from the **for each** block and adding a Text block containing a single space character

Although the counter value is numerical it gets copied into the concatenated string as a text value.

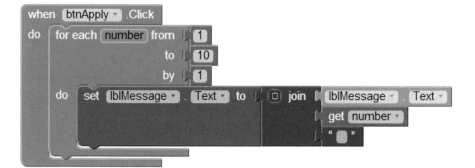

7 Run the app then tap the Button to see the concatenated string get written in the Label – listing the counter value on each iteration of this **for each** loop

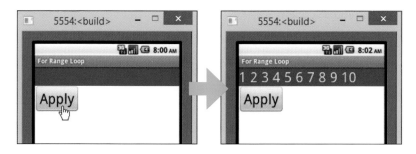

Click on the Viewer, then type "1" and hit Return to create a number **1** block. Click on the Viewer then type "text" and hit Return to create a **text** block.

61

Looping through a list

Programming loop structures in an Android App can also iterate through each item in a List using a **for each in list** loop, which executes its specified statements once for each item found in the List. This loop ends when it reaches the end of the List.

ForEach.apk

1 Start a new App Inventor project named "ForEach" then add a Label component and a Button component – naming the components **lblMessage** and **btnApply**

2 Launch the Blocks editor, then drag an **initialize global** block from the Built-in Variables drawer and name the variable "weekdays"

3 Snap in a **make a list** block from the Built-in Lists drawer and add Text blocks for each weekday

4 Add an event-handler for the button's Click event to the Viewer from the button's drawer

5 Snap in a **for each in list** block from the Built-in Control drawer – a loop argument named **item** is created automatically

6 Assign a reference to the variable to the loop by dragging a **get global weekdays** block from the **initialize global** block – to specify the list it contains

...cont'd

Next, add blocks stating what the loop should do on each iteration.

7 Drag in a **set lblMessage.Text** block and snap it into the **for each in list** block's **do** socket

8 From the Built-in Text drawer, add a **join** block to the **set lblMessage.Text** block – providing sockets to concatenate (join) values into a single text string

Hot tip

A List is also referred to as a variable "array", in which each item is an array "element".

9 Snap blocks into the **join** block to assign a text string to the Label on each iteration, by dragging a **get item** block from the **for each in list** block and adding a Text block containing a space character

10 Run the app then tap the Button to see the concatenated string get written on the Label – listing the List item value on each iteration of this **for each in list** loop

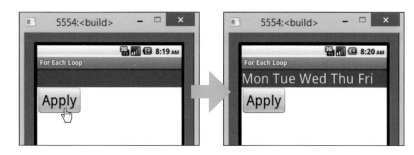

Don't forget

The first string assigned to the **join** block is the current value of the Label content.

Looping while true

An alternative to the **for each** loop is a **while** programming loop that allows an Android App to progress by repeatedly executing specified statements, but only while a test condition remains **true**. The **while** loop ends when the test condition becomes **false**.

While.apk

1 Start a new App Inventor project named "While" then add a Label component and a Button component – naming the components **lblMessage** and **btnApply**

2 Launch the Blocks editor, then drag an **initialize global** block from the Built-in Variables drawer – to act as an iteration counter

3 Name the variable **i** and set its initial value to number **10**

```
initialize global i to  10
```

4 Add an event-handler for the button's Click event and snap in a **while** block from the Built-in Control drawer

5 Add a test expression by inserting a ≥ block from the Built-in Math drawer, a **get global i** block from the **initialize global** block, and a Math number **1** block – testing if the counter is greater than zero

```
when btnApply .Click
do  while test    get global i  ≥  1
    do
```

Don't forget

The condition could alternatively be tested using the expression **>0**.

Next, add blocks stating what the loop should do on each iteration.

6 Drag in a **set lblMessage.Text** block from the label's drawer and snap it into the **while** block's **do** socket

7 From the Built-in Text drawer, add a **join** block to the **set lblMessage.Text** block – providing sockets to concatenate (join) values into a single text string

8 Assign a text string to the Label on each iteration, using a **get global i** block from the **initialize global** block and adding a Text block containing a space

Add a statement to change the counter value on each iteration.

9 From the **initialize global** block snap a **set global i** block below the **set lblMessage.Text** block

10 Insert a subtraction in the **to** socket using a - block from the Built-in Math drawer, a **get global i** block from the **initialize global** block, and a number **1** block

11 Run the app then tap the Button to see the Label display the counter value on each iteration of this **while** loop

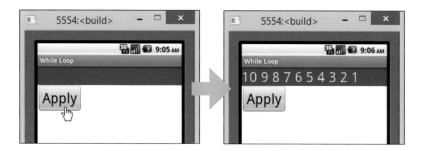

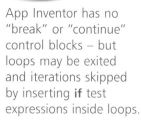

App Inventor has no "break" or "continue" control blocks – but loops may be exited and iterations skipped by inserting **if** test expressions inside loops.

A **while** loop is often more flexible than a **for each** loop as it tests for a Boolean value of **true** or **false**, rather than testing a numeric value.

Summary

- An application is a series of program instructions that tell the device what to do

- A statement is an instruction that performs a program task

- A procedure is a group of one or more statements that may be called upon at any time for execution by the program

- A variable is a container in which a numeric or text string value may be stored for subsequent use by the app

- An object is a fundamental program entity that has Property characteristics and Method actions

- The Math drawer provides **+ - x** and **/** arithmetic operators that perform numeric calculation, then return its numerical result

- The Math drawer provides comparison operators that perform numeric comparison, then return its Boolean **true** or **false** result

- The Logic drawer provides **and or** and **not** operators that perform Boolean comparison, then return its Boolean **true** or **false** result

- The Control drawer provides **if** and **if else** blocks that perform conditional branching by testing a given condition

- A Notifier component allows an app to interact with the user via Alert, Message, Choice, and Input dialogs

- The Control drawer provides **for each, for each in list**, and **while** blocks that repeatedly execute their statements in a loop

- A **for each** loop uses a counter to test the number of times it has executed its statements, and ends when it reaches the extreme of its specified range

- A **for each in list** loop executes its statements once for each item in a List, and ends when it reaches the end of that List

- A **while** loop executes its statements while a test condition remains **true**, and ends when that test condition becomes **false**

4 Calling functions

This chapter demonstrates how to group together statements into procedure structures that may be called to perform functions within an Android app.

Calling object methods

Application objects have "methods" that can be called upon to perform particular functions within the app. The method blocks can be found within their component's drawer in the Blocks editor and have some differences in the way they are used.

Many methods need information "arguments" to be supplied in the call, such as coordinates for a Canvas object's **DrawCircle** method.

Some methods also return a value to the caller when they are called. For example, a Canvas object's **GetPixelColor** method returns the color of a pixel at the specified location on the Canvas.

Other methods require no arguments and return nothing when called. For example, a Canvas object's **Clear** method simply clears the Canvas area and returns no value to the caller.

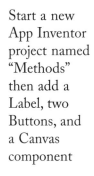

Methods.apk

Don't forget

The Text block shown here contains no text to specify an empty string.

 1 Start a new App Inventor project named "Methods" then add a Label, two Buttons, and a Canvas component

2 Launch the Blocks editor then drag in an event-handler for the first button's Click event from the button's drawer

3 From the Canvas component's drawer, snap in a call to its **Clear** method – to clear any Canvas content when called

```
when  btnClear  .Click
do   call  canEasel  .Clear
     set  lblMessage . Text  to  "   "
```

4 Add a statement to clear any Label content by assigning it an empty text string

Now, drag in an event-handler for the second button's Click event from its drawer

 Snap in a call to the Canvas object's **DrawCircle** method and specify three required arguments – to draw a 50-pixel radius circle when called at coordinates of X:50, Y:50

You can insert a **split color** block from the Built-in Colors drawer to translate the return from the **GetPixelColor** method into Red, Green, Blue, and Alpha components 0-255.

Hot tip

 Add a statement with a call to the Canvas object's **GetPixelColor** method – to write the numeric value of the Canvas's central pixel on the Label when called

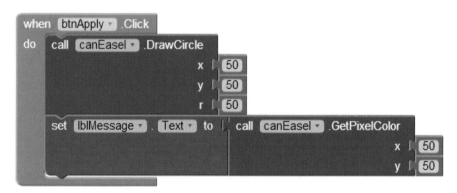

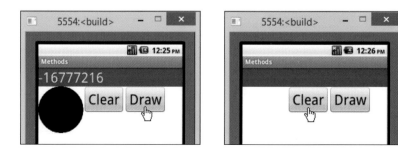 Run the app then tap the Buttons to see the Canvas methods draw a circle and write on the Label

Creating procedures

Multiple statements can be usefully grouped within a "procedure" to create a function with a name of your choice. The procedure can then be called upon by name to execute its statements.

As with object methods, described on the previous page, procedures can be created to accept arguments that pass data from the caller, and may also return a value to the caller, or may simply perform a task requiring no arguments and returning no value.

Procedure.apk

 Start a new App Inventor project named "Procedure" then add three Labels, a TextBox, and a Button component

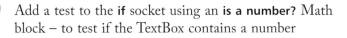

 Launch the Blocks editor then drag a **to** Procedures block onto the Viewer and edit its name to "cmToInches"

Next, snap an **if else** Control block into the procedure block

The Procedures drawer in App Inventor 2 replaces the "Definitions" drawer in the previous version.

Add a test to the **if** socket using an **is a number?** Math block – to test if the TextBox contains a number

to cmToInches
do   if   is a number?   txtCentimeters   Text
      then
      else

 Add a statement to the **else** socket – to write appropriate advice in the "?" Label when the test fails

set lblResult . Text to " Enter a valid number! "

6 Add a statement to the **then** socket – to write a computed value in the "?" Label when the test succeeds

`set lblResult . Text to ( ( txtCentimeters . Text / ( 2.54 )`

7 Insert a **format as decimal** Math block in the statement above – to ensure the computed value will always have two decimal places

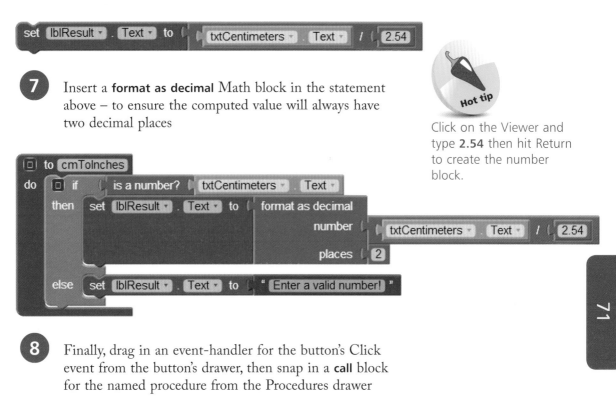

Hot tip

Click on the Viewer and type **2.54** then hit Return to create the number block.

8 Finally, drag in an event-handler for the button's Click event from the button's drawer, then snap in a **call** block for the named procedure from the Procedures drawer

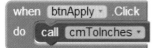

```
when btnApply .Click
do   call cmToInches
```

Hot tip

9 Run the app then input a value and tap the Button to see the procedure calls respond

As with variable naming, give meaningful names to your procedures. When you create a procedure a **call** block bearing its name gets automatically added to the Procedures drawer.

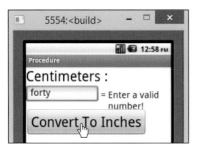

Passing arguments

The **to** Procedures block, described in the previous example, can be extended by clicking on the mutator button and adding an **input** socket to provide the ability to receive information when that procedure is called. The calling statement must supply the expected input. For example, a procedure with two inputs must be supplied with precisely two inputs ("arguments") when called.

1 Start a new App Inventor project named "Argument" then add two Labels, a TextBox, and a Button component

Argument.apk

2 Launch the Blocks editor then drag a **to** Procedures block onto the Viewer and edit its name to "greet"

3 Add an **input** to the **to** Procedures block and edit its name to "user"

Don't forget

As with variable names, the names given to inputs should be meaningful and unique within the procedure.

4 Snap in an **if else** Control block with a test using an **is empty** Text block, and drag in a **get user** block from the **to** Procedures block – to test if the TextBox is empty

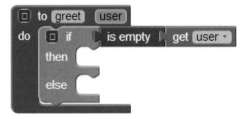

72

5 Add a statement to the **then** socket – to write appropriate advice in the Label when the test succeeds

6 Now, add a statement to the **else** socket – to write the argument value in the Label when the test fails

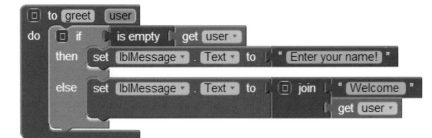

Beware

The **is empty** test will only succeed if the TextBox is completely empty – typing letters, numbers, or even space characters will see it fail.

7 Drag in an event-handler for the button's Click event from the button's drawer, then snap in a **call** block for the named procedure from the Procedures drawer – passing the TextBox contents as its sole argument

8 Run the app then input a value and tap the Button to see the procedure calls respond using the supplied argument

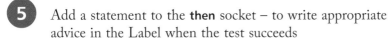

Hot tip

When you add an **input** you can click it to obtain **get** and **set** blocks to retrieve and store the value it contains.

Returning results

A procedure can usefully return a value to the caller. This is often desirable to return a **result** after the procedure has processed values passed to it as arguments. For example, a procedure created to perform arithmetic on two argument values.

Return.apk

1 Start a new App Inventor project named "Return" then add three Labels, two TextBoxes, and a Button component

2 Launch the Blocks editor then drag an **initialize global** Variables block onto the Viewer and edit its name

3 Drag in a **to result** Procedures block and add two **input** arguments then edit their names

The blocks have ! warning icons until the required blocks are snapped into their sockets.

4 Add an **if else** Control block with a test using an **and** Logic block, **is a number?** Math blocks, and **get** blocks from each input, into the **to** Procedures block – to test if both arguments are numeric

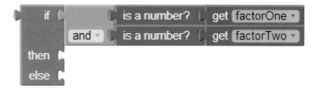

5 Snap a **do result** Control block statement into the **then** socket – to assign a value when the test succeeds

6 Snap another **do result** Control block statement into the **else** socket – to assign a message when the test fails

Hot tip

Notice that no blocks directly relating to the interface appear in the procedure – it is purely manipulating data.

7 Drag in an event-handler for the button's Click event from the button's drawer, then snap in a **call** block for the named procedure – passing both TextBox contents as arguments and assigning the returned value to the "?" Label

8 Run the app then input values and tap the Button to see the procedure calls respond with the returned value

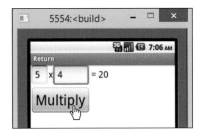

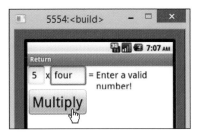

Ignoring results

Occasionally you may wish to call a procedure that returns a value to the caller, yet ignore the returned value. This will typically arise when the procedure is used by more than one app feature. For example, two buttons might call the same procedure but only one uses its returned value. App Inventor has an **evaluate but ignore result** Control block for this purpose.

Values to be stored for use only within a procedure can usefully be contained in a "local" variable, which is not accessible to other parts of the program.

Ignore.apk

1 Start a new App Inventor project named "Ignore" then add a Label, two Buttons, and a Clock component

2 Launch the Blocks editor then drag a **to result** Procedures block onto the Viewer and edit its name

3 Snap in an **initialize local** Variables block and set its initial value to be an empty string

Local variables were introduced in App Inventor 2. They allow like-named variables to appear in the same program if they are declared in separate procedures.

4 Add a **do result** Control block to the **in** socket that calls upon the Clock to return the current day of the week

5 Add an **if** test to the **in** socket – to write an appropriate message on the Label when the test succeeds

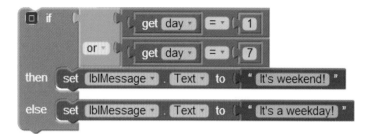

Hot tip

The clock's Weekday method returns a number from 1 (Sunday) to 7 (Saturday).

 6 Add an event-handler for the first button's Click event to write the procedure's return value on the Label

 7 Add an event-handler for the second button's Click event

8 Finally, add an **evaluate but ignore result** Control block and a call to the named procedure – that will ignore any returned value

```
when  btnIgnore  .Click
do    evaluate but ignore result    call  whatDay
```

NEW

App Inventor 2 added the **do result** and **evaluate but ignore result** Control blocks to the previous version.

9 Run the app then input values and tap the Buttons to see the procedure's return value get used and ignored

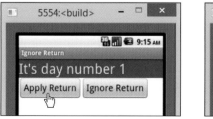

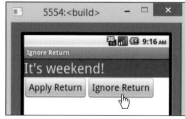

77

Calling subroutines

Procedures can be created for the express purpose of providing functionality for other procedures. This is considered to be good practice – as functionality is modularized into separate procedures. A procedure that is called from within another procedure is often referred to as "subroutine". For example, a procedure that returns a text string to its caller might itself call upon a subroutine to perform an arithmetical function.

Subroutine.apk

Don't forget

App Inventor insists that the two Math blocks must be nested as shown to determine operator precedence – as described on page 52.

1 Start a new App Inventor project named "Subroutine" then add a Label, a TextBox, and a Button component

	📶 🔋 9:48
Subroutine	
	Apply

2 Launch the Blocks editor then drag an **initialize global** Variables block onto the Viewer and edit its name

initialize global string to " "

3 Add a **to** Procedures block and create an input, then add Math **x** blocks to perform arithmetic on the input value – to complete a subroutine that returns its **result** cubed

to getCube n
result
do
result   get n × get n × get n

4 Drag in another **to** Procedures block and create an input, then add the variable as its return **result**

to buildString input
result
do
result   get global string

…cont'd

5 Snap an **if else** Control block into the second procedure block – to test if the passed argument is numeric

```
if    is a number?  get input
then
else
```

6 Add a statement to the **then** socket to build a string by employing the subroutine – to write an appropriate message on the Label when the test succeeds

```
set global string to    join  " Cubed is : "   call getCube n  get input
```

7 Add a statement to the **else** socket – to write an appropriate message on the Label when the test fails

```
set global string to  " Enter a valid number! "
```

Hot tip

Consider creating a subroutine if you find yourself repeating similar instructions in an app.

8 Finally, add an event-handler for the button's Click event – to write the subroutine's return value on the Label

```
when btnApply .Click
do  set lblMessage . Text to  call buildString
                              input  txtInput  Text
```

9 Run the app then input values and tap the Button to see the return value include the subroutine's return

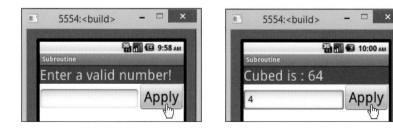

79

Validating input

Procedures can return Boolean values to the caller instead of text or numbers. This allows a procedure call to be used directly as a conditional test – where a **true** return will see the test succeed, and a **false** return will see it fail. For example, a procedure may be called upon to validate user input.

Validation.apk

1 Start a new App Inventor project named "Validation" then add a Label, a TextBox, and a Button component

 2 Launch the Blocks editor then drag an **initialize global** Variables block onto the Viewer and edit its name

 3 Add a **to** Procedures block that will return the current value of the variable to the caller

Hot tip

You can find the **contains text** block in the Text drawer.

 4 Snap in an **if** Control block to test whether the current TextBox value contains an "@" at character

5 Snap another **if** block into the **then** socket to test whether the TextBox value contains a "." period character – and to change the variable value when both tests succeed

Click on the Viewer area then type **true** and hit Return to create a Boolean block.

6 Add an event-handler for the button's Click event from the button's drawer – to set the variable's initial state

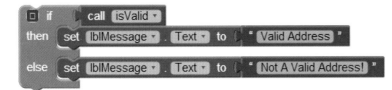

7 Snap in an **if else** Control block – to test if the variable state has changed after validation and write an appropriate message on the Label

8 Run the app then input an email address and tap the Button to see the validation result

 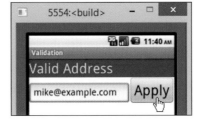

This example checks for the existence of an @ character and a period so does not provide extensive validation of the email format – but it could be made more comprehensive.

Doing mathematics

The App Inventor Math drawer provides typical mathematic functions that perform as you would expect. Additionally, it provides other less familiar functions that can also be useful. For example, to perform circle calculations, the constant value of Pi can be assigned to a variable by converting 180 degrees to radians.

Math.apk

 Start a new App Inventor project named "Math" then add two Labels, a TextBox, and a Button component

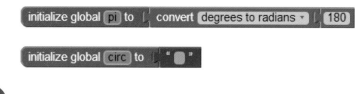

 Launch the Blocks editor then drag two **initialize global** Variables blocks onto the Viewer and edit their names

3 Add a **convert degrees to radians** Math block to assign Pi, and add an empty **text** block

initialize global (pi) to | convert (degrees to radians ▾) | 180

initialize global (circ) to | " ◯ "

 Add an event-handler for the button's Click event

 Snap in an **if else** Control block – to test if the input entered by the user is numeric

Hot tip

A radian is the ratio between the length of an arc and its radius. One radian is equal to 180/Pi degrees.

6 Add a statement to the **then** socket to assign a computed value to the empty variable, using Pi

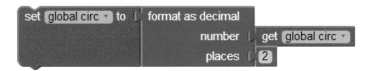

7 Add another statement to the **then** socket to ensure the computed value will always have two decimal places

A circle's circumference is calculated by multiplying Pi by its diameter (twice its radius).

8 Add a final statement to the **then** socket – to write an appropriate message on the Label when the test succeeds

9 Add a statement to the **else** socket – to write an appropriate message on the Label when the test fails

set lblMessage . Text to " Enter a valid number! "

10 Run the app then input a number and tap the Button to perform a mathematical calculation

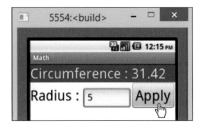

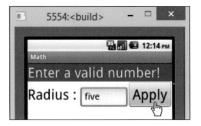

The value of Pi returned by converting 180 degrees to radians in this example is only correct to five decimal places – as 3.14159.

83

Generating random numbers

Random numbers can be generated using the Math **random integer** function. This returns an integer within a range specified by its two arguments. For example, arguments of one and 20 return a random integer within the range 1-20 inclusive.

Random.apk

1 Start a new App Inventor project named "Random" then add two Labels, a TextBox, and a Button component

🔋📶 9:48
Random Number
I have thought of a number between 1 and 20 - can you guess what it is?
Guess : ⬚ Apply

2 Launch the Blocks editor then drag an **initializ⌐** Variables block onto the Viewer and edit ⌐

initialize global num to 10

3 Add a **to** Procedures block to assign a ra⌐ the variable whenever the procedure gets c⌐

to getNumber
do set global num to random integer from 1 to 20

Hot tip

There is also a **random fraction** function that returns a value in the range 0-1 when called.

4 Call the procedure when the app first launches – to assign an initial random integer to the variable

when Screen1 Initialize
do call getNumber

5 Add a Click event-handler containing an **if else** Control – to test if an input number is greater than the stored random number, and write an appropriate message when it succeeds

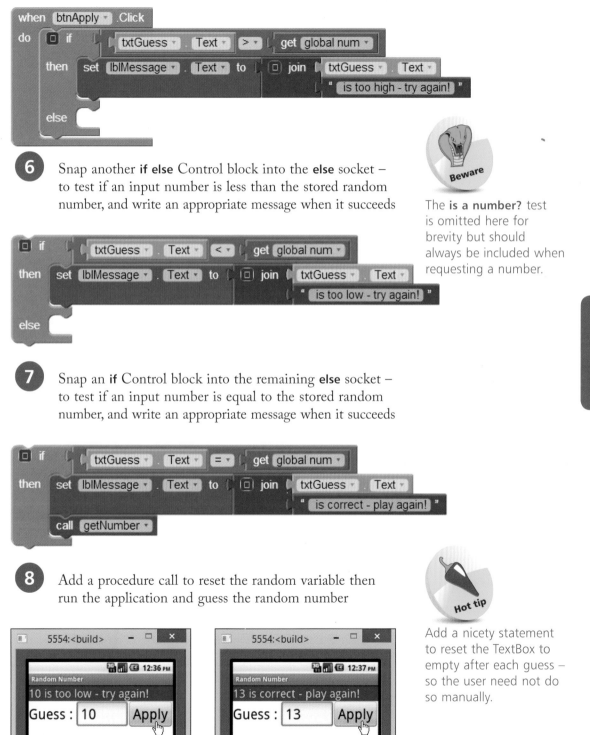

6 Snap another **if else** Control block into the **else** socket – to test if an input number is less than the stored random number, and write an appropriate message when it succeeds

Beware

The **is a number?** test is omitted here for brevity but should always be included when requesting a number.

7 Snap an **if** Control block into the remaining **else** socket – to test if an input number is equal to the stored random number, and write an appropriate message when it succeeds

85

8 Add a procedure call to reset the random variable then run the application and guess the random number

Hot tip

Add a nicety statement to reset the TextBox to empty after each guess – so the user need not do so manually.

Summary

- Application objects have methods that can be called to perform functions within an app

- Many methods require information to be passed to them as arguments in the call

- Some methods return a value to the caller

- A procedure contains statements to be executed whenever that procedure gets called

- Procedures can be created to accept arguments and return a value to the caller

- Input arguments and returns are optional as some procedures merely perform a function

- A procedure requiring input arguments must be supplied with the required number of arguments when it is called

- The value returned by a procedure is often the result of processing values supplied as arguments by the caller

- An **evaluate but ignore result** block allows a procedure to be called and its return value ignored

- Subroutines provide functionality for other procedures

- Procedures can return text values, numeric values, or Boolean values to the caller

- A conditional test can directly call a procedure that returns a Boolean value when it is called

- The constant value of Pi can be assigned to a variable using a Math function call to convert 180 degrees to radians

- Calling the Math random integer function returns a random number within a range specified by its arguments

5 Managing text

This chapter demonstrates how to manage text strings within an Android app.

Manipulating strings

The App Inventor Built-in Text drawer contains the blocks that provide functions to manipulate strings of text. The basic text block contains the empty string " " by default but this can, of course, be edited to contain any text string the app demands.

A string can be appended to another string by the **join** function. This adds the second given string onto the end of the first given string, concatenating them into a single united string.

Multiple strings can be concatenated into a single string by the **join** function. This joins all given strings together in order.

Join.apk

 1 Start a new App Inventor project named "Join" then add a Label, and a Button component

Don't forget

Click the mutator button on the **join** block to add more string sockets.

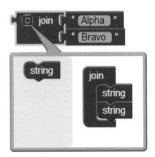

2 Launch the Blocks editor then drag an **initialize global** Variables block onto the Viewer and edit its name

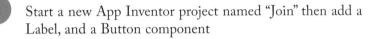

3 Add a third socket to the **join** block then snap simple Text string blocks in to build a concatenated string

4 Add another **initialize global** Variables block with a **join** block then build a second concatenated string

 5 Create an appending statement with a **join** block – ready to assign a united string to the Label

App Inventor 2 has a **join** block in place of the **make text** block in the previous version.

 6 Drag an event-handler for the button's Click event onto the Viewer from the button's drawer

 7 Snap in the appending statement and add both the named variable blocks

8 Run the app then tap the Button to see the concatenated string get written on the Label

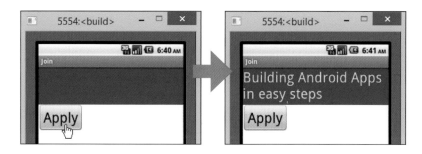

Include a space character after the word in each text block so they will be separated when united.

Querying strings

The Text drawer provides functions that can be used to query strings of text to discover their length and to discover whether they contain a specified piece of text.

A **length** function returns an integer that is the total number of characters within a given string, including space characters.

The **contains** function returns a Boolean value of **true** if a specified piece of text is contained in a specified string of text, otherwise it returns **false**.

A TextBox component can usefully be tested with an **is empty** function that returns **true** if it's empty, otherwise it returns **false**.

Query.apk

1 Start a new App Inventor project named "Query" then add a Label, a TextBox, and a Button component

Hot tip

Click on the Viewer and type "text" then hit Return to see a default **text** block appear.

2 Launch the Blocks editor then drag in an event-handler for the button's Click event from the button's drawer

3 Snap in an **if else** Control block to test if the TextBox is empty with an **is empty** Text block

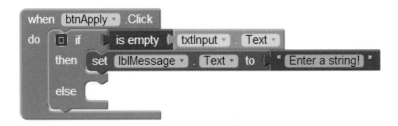

4 Add a statement in the **then** socket – to write a warning message on the Label when the test succeeds

5 Snap an **if else** Control block into the **else** socket to test if the TextBox contains "Java" with a **contains** Text block

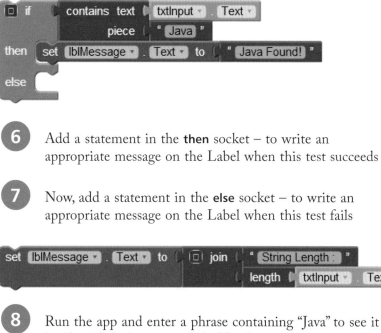

6 Add a statement in the **then** socket – to write an appropriate message on the Label when this test succeeds

7 Now, add a statement in the **else** socket – to write an appropriate message on the Label when this test fails

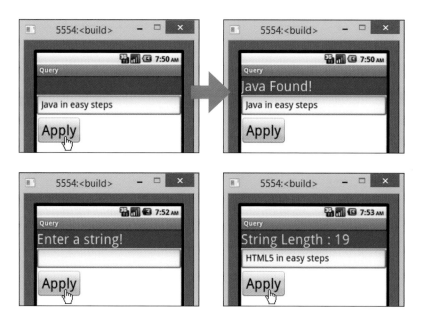

8 Run the app and enter a phrase containing "Java" to see it be identified, then amend the TextBox contents to see the other messages

Comparing strings

The Text drawer provides functions that can be used to compare text strings to determine their alphabetical order. Interestingly, this is achieved by totalling the ASCII code value of each character in the string and noting their order. Uppercase letters A-Z have code values in the range 65-90 whereas lowercase letters a-z have code values in the range 97-122. The total code value and character order will determine the alphabetical order of the strings.

When two identical text strings are compared by the **compare =** function their totals are the same so the function returns **true**. The **compare <** function only returns **true** when the first string total is <u>less than</u> that of the second string. Conversely, the **compare >** function only returns **true** when the first string total is <u>greater than</u> that of the second string.

Compare.apk

Don't forget

In comparisons character order is taken into account – so comparing "za" to "az" reveals that "za" has a greater total. In terms of ASCII values 'a' is 97 and 'z' is 122.

1 Start a new App Inventor project named "Compare" then add a Label, two TextBox components, and a Button

	📶 🔋 9:48
Compare	

Apply

2 Launch the Blocks editor then drag in an event-handler for the button's Click event from the button's drawer

3 Snap in an **if else** Control block that makes a **compare =** comparison between the TextBox contents – and writes an appropriate message on the Label when they match

4 Snap an **if else** Control block into the **else** socket – to make a **compare <** test between the TextBox contents

5 Add a statement in the **then** socket – to write an appropriate message on the Label when this test succeeds

6 Add a statement in the **else** socket – to write an appropriate message on the Label when this test fails

7 Run the app and enter text into both TextBoxes, then tap the Button to compare the strings

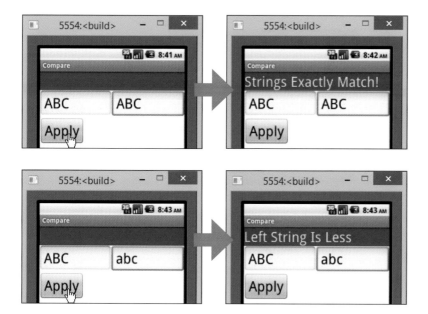

Trimming strings

The Text drawer provides useful functions to prepare text strings before making a comparison. Any leading or trailing spaces can be removed by the **trim** function. This returns a copy of the string with surrounding spaces removed and is useful to ignore extra spaces that the user may have entered.

A string can be converted to all lowercase by the **downcase** function, or converted to all uppercase by the **upcase** function. These return a converted copy of the string and are useful to allow the user to ignore case when entering text for comparison.

Trim.apk

 Start a new App Inventor project named "Trim" then add a Label, a TextBox, and a Button component

 Launch the Blocks editor then drag an **initialize global** Variables block onto the Viewer and edit its name

initialize global string to " "

Don't forget

You can check that the user has entered something into the TextBox with the **is text empty?** function.

3 Add an event-handler for the button's Click event that copies the TextBox contents into the variable

```
when btnApply .Click
do  set global string to  txtInput . Text
```

4 Now, add a statement within the event-handler to remove leading or trailing spaces from the string in the variable

set global string to trim get global string

5 Add another statement within the event-handler to convert the string in the variable to lowercase

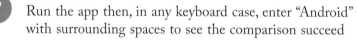

6 Finally, within the event-handler add an **if else** Control block to compare the string in the variable to "android" – and write an appropriate message in the Label

Beware

Quote marks are for descriptive purposes only – they are not part of the text strings.

7 Run the app then, in any keyboard case, enter "Android" with surrounding spaces to see the comparison succeed

8 Introduce intermediate space characters, or any other text, to see the comparison fail

Hot tip

Always trim spaces from around strings that have been input by the user.

Splitting strings

The Text drawer provides several functions to split text strings in a variety of ways. Most straightforward of these is **split at spaces** that splits a space-separated text string into individual pieces. These are returned as a list that can be stored in a variable.

An alternative delimiter to a space, such as a comma, can be specified to the **split** function. A comma-separated text string will be returned as a list of pieces, without the comma characters.

A text string can be simply split into two pieces by the **split at first** function, which splits a string around the first occurrence of a specified delimiter. For example, a comma-separated text string will be returned as the first piece and the remainder of the string.

Multiple alternative delimiters can be specified to the **split at any** function and the **split at first of any** function. These both separate a text string around any of their specified delimiters.

 1 Start a new App Inventor project named "Split" then add a Label, a TextBox, and a Button component

Split.apk

A "delimiter" is a character used to specify a boundary between regions of text.

 2 Launch the Blocks editor then drag an **initialize global** Variables block onto the Viewer and edit its name

initialize global **list** to " "

3 Add an event-handler for the button's Click event – to store a list split from user input within the variable

when **btnApply** .Click
do set **global list** to split at spaces **txtInput** . Text

...cont'd

4 Add a statement to the event-handler to clear the TextBox

set [lblMessage ▾] . [Text ▾] to (" [ ] "

5 Now, add a **for each** Control block to the event-handler –
to loop through the list of words stored in the variable

for each [item] in list (get [global list ▾]
do

Remember that the loop
variable is <u>named</u> at the
start of the **for each**
block, then its <u>value</u> is
used inside the loop.

6 Snap into the **do** socket a statement to write each list
piece on the Label, followed by a | pipe character

set [lblMessage ▾] . [Text ▾] to (▣ join ([lblMessage ▾] . [Text ▾]
get [item ▾]
" [ ] "

7 Run the app then enter a space-separated string to see
the list of pieces get written on the Label

You can write a newline
onto a Label by adding a
\n escape sequence in a
text block.

Extracting substrings

The Text drawer provides functions that can be used to extract a section from within a string – returning it as a "substring".

A string can be searched for a specified substring using the **starts at** function. This returns an integer that is the substring's first character position in the string, or zero if the search fails. For example, the substring "cut" is found in "Calcutta" at 4.

Specifying the position of a character within a string to the **segment** function, together with a length value, returns a substring that begins at the specified position and is of the specified length.

Multiple occurrences of a substring within a string can all be replaced with a specified alternative by the **replace all** function.

Extract.apk

 Start a new App Inventor project named "Extract" then add a Label, a TextBox, and a Button component

Hot tip

Notice how the **downcase** function is used here to allow a case-insensitive search.

 Launch the Blocks editor then drag an **initialize global** Variables block onto the Viewer and edit its name

initialize global position to 0

3 Add an event-handler for the button's Click event to store the starting position of a substring in the variable

when btnApply .Click
do set global position to starts at text downcase txtInput . Text
piece " and "

...cont'd

4 Add within the event-handler an **if else** Control block to test whether the substring has been located

If the variable maintains its initial zero value the **starts at** search has not found the substring.

5 Now, add a statement to the **then** socket – to write the substring on the Label when the test succeeds

6 Add a statement to the **else** socket – to write an appropriate message on the Label when the test fails

7 Run the app then enter a string and search for the substring to see the extracted substring get written on the Label when it is found within your string

This search will succeed at the first position it finds the "and" substring – in any string word.

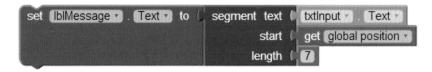

Summary

- The App Inventor Built-in Text drawer contains the blocks that provide functions to manipulate strings of text

- A string can be appended to another string by the **join** function

- Multiple strings can be concatenated into a single string by the **join** function

- The **length** function returns the size of a string including spaces

- The **contains** function returns **true** if a specified piece of text is found within a string

- TextBox contents can be tested by the **is empty** Text block

- Comparison of two strings' alphabetical order can be made by the **compare <**, **compare >**, and **compare =** functions

- The **trim** function removes surrounding spaces around a string

- A lowercase copy of a string is returned by the **downcase** function, whereas **upcase** returns an uppercase copy of a string

- The **split at spaces** function splits a space-separated string into a list of individual pieces

- The **split** function returns a list of separated string pieces excluding the specified delimiter

- The **split at first** function splits a string into two pieces around the first occurrence of a specified delimiter

- Multiple alternative delimiters can be specified to the **split at any** function and the **split at first of any** function

- The **starts at** function returns the first character position of a substring within a string or zero if the search fails

- The **segment** function returns a substring that begins at a specified string position and is of a specified length

- Multiple occurrences of a substring within a string can all be replaced by the **replace all** function

6 Handling lists

This chapter demonstrates how to create lists and how to handle list items within an Android app.

Making lists

The App Inventor Built-in Lists drawer contains the blocks that provide functions to create "lists" and to manipulate list items. A list is a series of items that can be assigned to a variable – so the variable can store multiple values, instead of just a single value.

The **make a list** block provides sockets that can accept either Text blocks or Math basic number blocks to define the list item values. The **make a list** block can be expanded by clicking on its mutator button to provide further sockets in which to define subsequent list item values.

Assigning a variable that contains a list to a Label component will display all the values as a space-separated list.

List.apk

1 Start a new App Inventor project named "List" then add a Label, and a Button component

2 Launch the Blocks editor then drag an **initialize global** Variables block onto the Viewer and edit its name

initialize global (list) to

3 Snap in a **make a list** block from the Lists drawer

initialize global (list) to ▢ make a list

4 Click on the **make a list** block's mutator button and add a third socket – ready to make a list of three items

An AppInventor "list" is also known as a variable "array" in other programming languages.

 5 Snap in three Text blocks to define the list items

initialize global **list** to | make a list " Red "
" Green "
" Blue "

103

 6 Add an event-handler for the button's Click event then snap in a statement to display the complete list

when **btnApply** .Click
do set **lblMessage** . **Text** to | get **global list**

The values appear enclosed within parentheses to identify them as list items.

 7 Run the app then tap the Button to see the list items appear as a space-separated list within parentheses

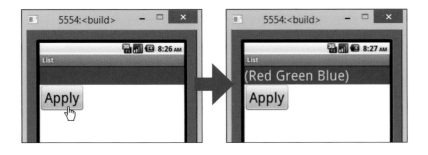

Querying lists

The Lists drawer provides several functions to query lists in a variety of ways. Most straightforward is the **is a list?** function that returns a Boolean **true** or **false** value to determine whether a specified variable does indeed contain a list. Similarly, the **is list empty?** function will identify an empty list and the **is in list?** function will seek a specified value, returning a Boolean result.

Usefully, a list's length can be discovered by the **length of list** function, which returns an integer that is the number of items in the specified list.

Items in a list have indexed position numbers, the first item at position 1. A particular item can be sought in a list by the **index in list** function, which returns an integer that is the index number of that item in the specified list.

QueryList.apk

1 Start a new App Inventor project named "QueryList" then add a Label, and a Button component

The creation of this list is described in the example on the previous page.

2 Launch the Blocks editor then drag an **initialize global** Variables block onto the Viewer and create a list of three Text items

...cont'd

3 Add an event-handler for the button's Click event – that tests whether the variable does indeed contain a list

4 Now, add a test to this **then** socket – to see if a particular item exists

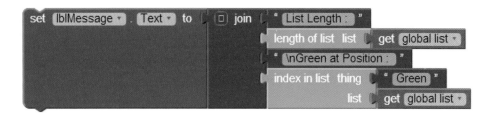

It is good practice to first test for the existence of a non-empty list before querying items to prevent errors.

5 Add a statement to this second **then** socket to write a two-line message on the Label

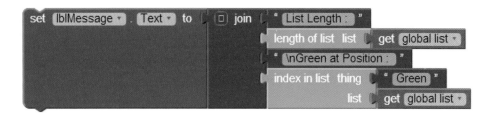

6 Run the app then tap the Button to see the list length and the list index position of the specified item

The **index in list** function returns zero if the specified thing is not found in the list.

105

Adding list items

The Lists drawer provides several functions to add items to a list. An item can be inserted into a list at a particular position by the **insert list item** function, which specifies the value to be inserted and the index position at which it is to be inserted.

One or more single items can be tacked onto the end of a list starting after the final index position by the **add items to list** function, and a list can be appended to another list using the **append to list** function.

Add.apk

1 Start a new App Inventor project named "Add" then add a Label, and a Button component

> Add Items
>
> **Apply**
>
> 🛜 📶 🔋 9:48

2 Launch the Blocks editor then drag two **initialize global** Variables blocks onto the Viewer and edit their names

3 Snap **make a list** Lists blocks into the variable blocks, then add Text and Math number blocks to create two lists

Hot tip

The **make a list** function can be used to create an empty list to which items can be added later.

initialize global (letters) to ▸ □ make a list " A "
" B "
" C "

initialize global (numbers) to ▸ □ make a list 1
2
3

4 Add an event-handler for the button's Click event then snap in an **insert list item** block – to insert a " & " list item at index position 3

The **append to list** function is used to append a list, not a single item.

5 Snap into the event-handler an **add items to list** block – to add a single " + " item at the end of a list

```
add items to list   list   get global letters
              item   " + "
```

6 Snap into the event-handler an **append to list** block – to add one list at the end of the other

```
append to list   list1   get global letters
                 list2   get global numbers
```

7 Snap into the event-handler a statement to display the modified list then run the app and tap the button to see the result

```
set lblMessage . Text to   get global letters
```

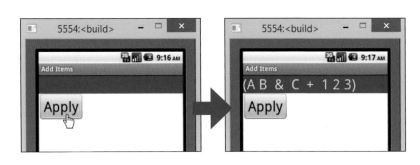

The + symbol appended as text is simply a character, not an arithmetical operator.

107

Selecting items

The Lists drawer provides a **select list item** function that selects a list item at a specified index position. This can, of course, be used to select a single list item but it can also be used within a loop to select several list items – by incrementing the index number in each iteration of the loop.

Select.apk

 Start a new App Inventor project named "Select" then add a Label, and a Button component

The first item in a list index is at position 1. Other programming languages begin index numbering at zero.

2 Launch the Blocks editor then drag an **initialize global** Variables block onto the Viewer and create an alphabetically ordered list of text items

3 Drag a second **initialize global** Variables block onto the Viewer and create an empty list – to store selected items

initialize global `third` to ◀ ▣ create empty list

4 Add an event-handler for the button's Click event and snap in a loop – iterating through the text list by steps of 3

```
when btnApply .Click
do   for each number from  3
                       to  length of list list  get global union
                       by  3
     do
```

Notice how the **length of list** function is used here to specify when the loop should end.

5 Snap into the **do** socket a statement to select each third item from the text list and add it to the empty list

```
add items to list   list   get global third
                    item   select list item list  get global union
                                         index  get number
```

6 Add a final statement to the event-handler to display the items selected by the loop

```
set lblMessage . Text to  get global third
```

7 Run the app and tap the Button to see the list of selected items appear on the Label

Swapping items

The Lists drawer provides a **remove list item** function that removes an item from a list. Subsequent items in the list then adopt new position numbers by shuffling down the index. For example, removing an item at index position 2 means that the item at index position 3 adopts index position 2, and so on.

A list item may also be replaced with a new value using the **replace list item** function, which retains the same index position.

Swap.apk

 Start a new App Inventor project named "Swap" then add a Label, and a Button component

![Screenshot showing Swap Items app with Apply button]

 Launch the Blocks editor then drag an **initialize global** Variables block onto the Viewer and create a list

```
initialize global colors to   make a list " Red "
                                            " Lime "
                                            " Teal "
                                            " Blue "
```

3 Add an event-handler for the screen's Initialize event then snap in a statement to display the initial list items

```
when Screen1 .Initialize
do   set lblMessage . Text to   get global colors
```

4 Add an event-handler for the button's Click event and snap in a statement to remove the third list item

The **Screen1.Initialize** block is located in the **Screen1** drawer.

5 Now, add a statement to this event-handler to replace the value of the second list item

6 Add a final statement to this event-handler to display the list items once more

 set lblMessage . Text to get global colors

7 Run the app to see the initial list items appear on the Label, then tap the button to see the modified list

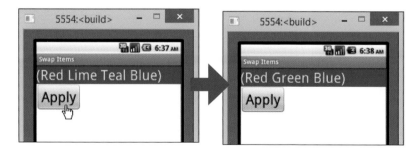

111

Manipulating lists

The Lists drawer provides a **copy list** function that copies an entire list into another variable. It also provides a **pick a random item** function that randomly selects an item from a specified list.

App Inventor usefully has a Built-in Colors drawer that provides blocks of standard colors that can be used as list items.

 Manipulate.apk

1 Start a new App Inventor project named "Manipulate" then add a Label, and a Button component

> 📶 🔋 9:48
>
> Manipulate Items
>
> **Apply**

2 Launch the Blocks editor then drag two **initialize global** Variables blocks onto the Viewer and create two lists – of Colors blocks and their corresponding names

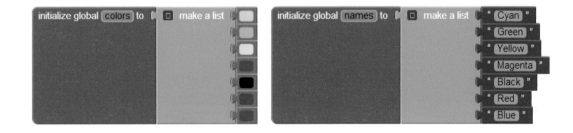

3 Drag another **initialize global** Variables block onto the Viewer – to store the current selected index position

> initialize global position to (1)

The actual values of the Color blocks are numeric but have color swatches for easy recognition.

4 Add an event-handler for the button's Click event to set the Label's background color from a random selection

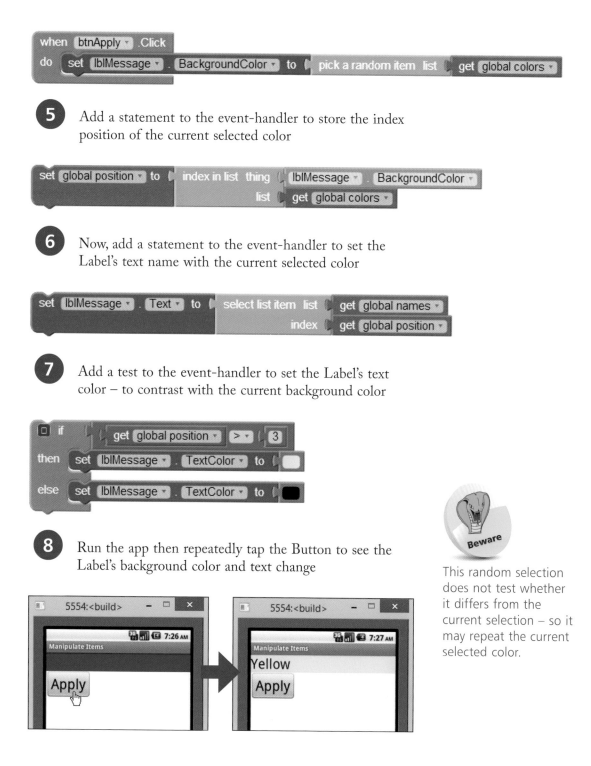

5 Add a statement to the event-handler to store the index position of the current selected color

6 Now, add a statement to the event-handler to set the Label's text name with the current selected color

7 Add a test to the event-handler to set the Label's text color – to contrast with the current background color

8 Run the app then repeatedly tap the Button to see the Label's background color and text change

Beware

This random selection does not test whether it differs from the current selection – so it may repeat the current selected color.

Separating lists

The Lists drawer provides functions to separate lists into a string of comma-separated values (CSV). Most straightforward of these is the **list to csv row** function that returns the list items as a comma-separated string with each item surrounded by double quotes. Similarly, the **list to csv table** function returns the list items as a comma-separated string with each item surrounded by double quotes, but also separates each item by a CRLF carriage return. Conversely, a list can be created from a comma-separated string assigned to a variable by the **list from csv row** function. Additionally, a list can be created from a comma-separated list that also separates each item by a CRLF carriage return (in table format) by the **list from csv table** function.

Separate.apk

 Start a new App Inventor project named "Separate" then add a Label, and two Button components

A returned CSV row does not have a CRLF carriage return at the row end.

 Launch the Blocks editor then drag an **initialize global** Variables block onto the Viewer and create a list

 Add an event-handler for the screen's Initialize event then snap in a statement to display the initial list items

4 Add an event-handler for the first button's Click event – to display the list items as a comma-separated row

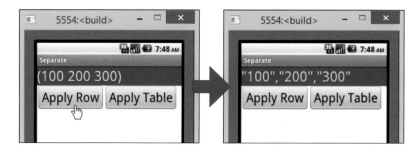

5 Now, add an event-handler for the second button's Click event – to display the list items as a comma-separated table, with each row separated by CRLF carriage returns

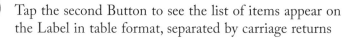

6 Run the app to see the list appear on the Label, then tap the first Button to see the comma-separated list of items

7 Tap the second Button to see the list of items appear on the Label in table format, separated by carriage returns

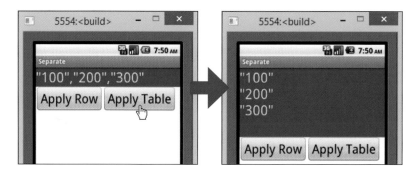

Don't forget

A returned CSV table does not have a CRLF carriage return at the end of each row.

Summary

- A list is a series of items that can be assigned to a variable so the variable can store multiple values

- The **make a list** block provides sockets that can accept Text blocks or Math number blocks to define the list item values

- Variables can be queried by the **is a list?** and **is list empty?** functions that return Boolean values of **true** or **false**

- The **length of list** and **index in list** functions return an integer value specifying list length and index position

- An item can be inserted into a list at a particular position by the **insert list item** function

- Single items can be added to a list by the **add items to list** function and another list can be added by **append to list**

- The **select list item** function selects a list item at a specified index position and can be used in a loop to select several items

- The **remove list item** function removes a list item at a specified index position

- A list item can be replaced using the **replace list item** function to specify an index position and a replacement value

- The **copy list** function copies an entire list into another variable

- A item can be randomly selected from a specified list using the **pick a random item** function

- The **list to csv row** function returns list items as a comma-separated string with each item surrounded by double quotes

- The **list to csv table** function returns list items as a comma-separated string with each item surrounded by double quotes and also separated by CRLF carriage returns

- Comma-separated strings can be converted to lists using the **list from csv row** function and **list from csv table** function

7 Embracing media

This chapter describes how to incorporate media resources and animation in an Android app.

Playing sounds

The App Inventor Media components palette provides a Player component that can be used to play audio files. Typically, these will be in the popular MP3 file format but Android also supports other audio formats, such as MIDI, WAV, and Vorbis.

A Player component is not visible on the interface but has **Start**, **Pause**, and **Stop** methods, with which to control audio playback, and a **Source** property to specify the audio resource to be played. An audio file must be added to the app as a Media resource, in much the same way that images are added to an app.

Sound.apk

1 Start a new App Inventor project named "Sound" then add three Button components to the interface

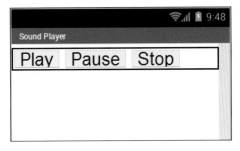

2 Open the Media palette then drag a non-visible Player and a non-visible Sound component to the interface

Hot tip

The audio resource automatically appears in the Media column after it has been uploaded.

3 Select the Sound component in the Components column then in the Properties column upload an audio file to set as its source to be played

4 Launch the Blocks editor then add an event-handler for the screen's Initialize event to specify the audio Sound as the Player component's Source – ready for playback

Tap the Play button to resume playback from the point it was paused, or from the start after it was stopped.

 5 Add event-handlers for the first two button's Click events, to Start and Pause playback of the audio resource

 6 Now, add an event-handler for the third button's Click event to Stop playback of the audio resource, and to again specify the Sound resource as the Player's source – ready for playback once more

119

 7 Run the app then tap the Buttons to Play, Pause, and Stop playback of the specified audio resource

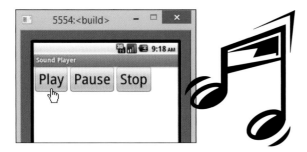

Use the Player component to play long sound files but you can use the Sound component alone for short sound files, such as sound effects.

Playing video

The App Inventor Media components palette provides a Video Player component that can be used to play video files. Android supports the MPEG-4 file format, as well as 3GPP and WMV file formats, but limits the video file size to 1Mb.

A Video Player component appears as a rectangle in the interface. The familiar media controls appear when the user taps the rectangle and are used to call its **Start**, **Pause**, and **SeekTo** methods, to control the video playback. The Video Player component also provides a **Source** property to specify the video resource to play.

A video file must be added to the app as a Media resource, in much the same way that images are added to an app.

Video.apk

1 Start a new App Inventor project named "Video" then add two Button components to the interface

Video Player	📶 🔋 9:48

Play Pause

2 Open the Media palette and drag a Video Player component to the interface

Media

🎥 Camcorder ⑦

📷 Camera ⑦

🖼 ImagePicker ⑦

▷ Player ⑦

🔊 Sound ⑦

● SoundRecorder ⑦

🎙 SpeechRecognizer ⑦

💬 TextToSpeech ⑦

🎬 VideoPlayer   ⑦

Y YandexTranslate ⑦

3 Click the Upload File button under the Media column and select a video file to upload – see it get added to the Media components list

Media

sample.mp4

Upload File ...

Hot tip

Video and Sound source files can be specified to players in the Designer or in the Blocks editor.

4 With the Video Player component selected, click the empty Source field in its Properties column and choose a video file resource as its source – ready for playback

Source

None
sample.mp4

Upload File ...

Cancel   OK

5 Launch the Blocks editor then add event-handlers for the two button's Click events, to Start and Pause playback

when btnPlay .Click
do call VideoPlayer1 .Start

when btnPause .Click
do call VideoPlayer1 .Pause

6 Run the app then tap the buttons to Play and Pause playback of the specified video resource

Don't forget

You can also tap the Video block area to reveal the controls to Play and Pause playback.

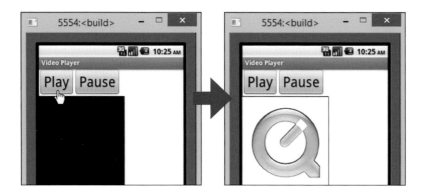

Snapping photos

The App Inventor Media components palette provides a Camera component that can interact with a device's camera interface.

A Camera component is not visible on the app interface but has **TakePicture** and **AfterPicture** methods, to snap a photo and to specify an action to perform afterwards.

Photos taken with the **TakePicture** method get added to the device's gallery, just like other photos taken by the camera.

Camera.apk

1 Start a new App Inventor project named "Camera" then add a single Button component to the interface

Camera
Snap A Photo

2 Open the Media components palette and drag a non-visible Camera component to the interface

Media

- Camcorder
- Camera
- ImagePicker
- Player
- Sound

Hot tip

The Camera component gets added to the Non-visible Components list that appears below the designer Viewer.

3 Launch the Blocks editor then add an event-handler for the button's Click event and snap in a call to the **TakePicture** method from the Camera's drawer

when btnSnap .Click
do call Camera1 .TakePicture

4 Add a call to the **AfterPicture** method from the Camera drawer to use the photo as the app's background

 5 Click the Build > App option in the App Inventor menu and download the app to your computer

Build ▾   Help ▾

App (provide QR code for .apk)

App (save .apk to my computer)

Installation of the app may require you to use the appropriate management software for your Android device – such as HTC Sync seen here for HTC phones.

Don't forget

 6 Connect your device to the computer and install the app on the device – as described on pages 22-23

All Apps

Adobe Reade Angry Birds Books Calculator
Calendar Call History Camcorder Camera
Camera Clock Downloads Facebook

123

7 Run the app then tap the Button to snap a photo and set it as the app's background

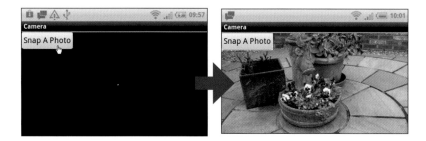

Hot tip

MyPhone Explorer is free phone management software for your computer available from Google Play Store and FJ Software at **fjsoft.at**

Picking images

The App Inventor Media components palette provides an ImagePicker component to select images from the device's gallery.

An ImagePicker component is not visible on the app interface but has an **AfterPicking** method to specify an action to perform after an image has been selected.

The selection of an image assigns the location of that image to the ImagePicker component's ImagePath property, and this can be used to specify the image as a background.

Picker.apk

1 Start a new App Inventor project named "Picker" then add a single ImagePicker component to the interface from the Media palette – the component provides a special button on the interface

Media	
📹 Camcorder	⑦
📷 Camera	⑦
🖼 ImagePicker	⑦
▷ Player	⑦
🔊 Sound	⑦

📶 📶 🔋 9:48

Picker

Pick An Image

Hot tip

An ImagePicker component also has **BeforePicking**, **GotFocus**, and **LostFocus** methods.

2 Launch the Blocks editor then add an event-handler from the ImagePicker's drawer to call its **AfterPicking** method to set the screen background to the selected image

```
when  ImagePicker1 . AfterPicking
do   set  Screen1 . BackgroundImage  to   ImagePicker1 . Selection
```

...cont'd

 Click the Build > App option in the App Inventor menu and download the app to your computer

 Connect your device to the computer and install the app on the device – as described on pages 22-23

Hot tip

Set the initial Screen Background color to None so the background image will fill the entire screen area.

 Run the app then select an image from your device's gallery to become the app background

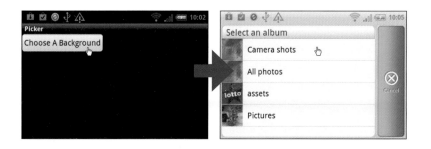

Don't forget

The selected image becomes the background of the app, not the home screen background.

Switching screens

App Inventor supports multiple Screen components in each app. Multi–screen apps are useful to provide individual forms on each screen that the user can switch between. The Blocks editor allows instructions for each screen to be assembled separately – almost as if they were each an individual app.

 Start a new App Inventor project named "Screens" then add two Button components to the Screen1 interface

Screens.apk

 Click the Add Screen button on the toolbar then add a Label and a Button component to the Screen2 interface

 Launch the Blocks editor and see it is ready to create instructions for Screen2

 Add an event-handler for the button's Click event and snap in a call to the **close screen** function from the Built-in Control drawer

App Inventor 2 lets you add screens in both Designer and Blocks mode – unlike the previous version that required you to be in Designer mode.

5 Click the Screen2 toolbar button to reveal a dropdown menu, then select the Screen1 option to switch the Blocks editor – ready to create instructions for Screen1

Hot tip

Media content can be added to each vertical screen to be "in focus" when their containing screen is visible.

6 Add an event-handler for the first button's Click event then snap in a call to the **open another screen** function from the Control drawer and a Text block of its name

7 Add an event-handler for the second screen button's Click event and snap in a call to the **close application** function from the Control drawer

 8 Run the app then tap the buttons to switch between the screens or close the app

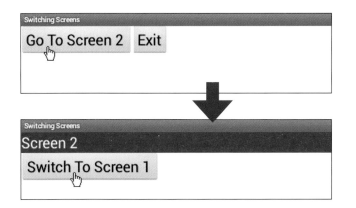

127

Beware

At the time of writing the **close application** control is not supported during development.

Animating components

The App Inventor Drawing and Animation palette provides a Ball component and an ImageSprite component that can be animated. The Ball is a sprite component, which is a filled disc that looks like a ball, but the ImageSprite component displays a specified image. Both these components must be contained within a Canvas component and can react to other sprites and to the Canvas edges.

A sprite's movement is specified by its properties. For example, to have a ball move 5 pixels toward the top of a canvas every 500 milliseconds (half second), you can set the Speed property to 5, the Interval property to 500, the Heading property to 90 (degrees), and the Enabled property to True.

When a sprite hits the edge of the Canvas an EdgeReached event occurs that numerically recognizes which edge has been reached.

Edge:	Value:
North	1
NorthEast	2
East	3
SouthEast	4
South	-1
SouthWest	-2
West	-3
NorthWest	-4

The edge value can then be passed to the sprite's Bounce method to reverse its direction of movement.

Animation.apk

1 Start a new App Inventor project named "Animation" then add a Canvas and a Ball component to the interface

2 Select the Ball component and set its physical properties to PaintColor Red, Radius 20, and check Visible

3 Set the Ball's movement properties to Speed 15, Interval 100, Heading 25, and check Enabled

...cont'd

 4 Set the Ball's initial coordinate properties to X 25, Y 25, and Z 1.0

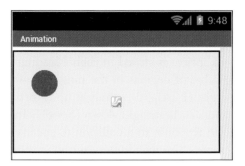

Hot tip

The ball's properties can alternatively be set by assigning values in the Blocks editor.

 5 Launch the Blocks editor then add an event-handler for the ball's EdgeReached event – an edge argument is automatically created

 6 Snap in a call to the ball's Bounce method and specify the value of the edge as its argument

 7 Run the app to see the Ball bounce around the Canvas

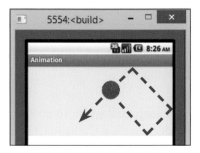

Don't forget

The value of opposite edges have reversed polarity so the Bounce method simply negates the reported edge value to reverse the direction.

Detecting collisions

An animated sprite can be made to react to another animated sprite when their movements collide on the Canvas. At the moment of collision a CollidedWith event occurs. The sprite's CollidedWith event-handler specifies the other sprite as its argument and can be used to change direction of both sprites.

The current direction of sprites is stored in their Heading property as a numeric value of degrees in the range 0-360. Zero is horizontally to the right (East), 90 is straight up (North), 180 is to the left (West), and 270 is straight down (South). These values can be changed in response to a collision to specify a new direction in which to move. Simply adding a numeric value to the current Heading will specify a new direction. In order to ensure the new value does not exceed 360 it is necessary to use the modulo operator. For example, (270+120=390) modulo 360=30.

Collide.apk

1 Start a new App Inventor project named "Collide" then add a Canvas and two Ball components to the interface, and set their properties as those in the previous example

The blue Ball sprite must be repositioned so it has a different starting point to that of the red Ball.

2 Launch the Blocks editor then add an event-handler for the screen's Initialize event to reposition the blue Ball sprite

```
when  Screen1 . Initialize
do    set  ballBlue . Y . to   125
```

3 Add event-handlers for each Ball sprite to reverse their direction when they collide with a Canvas edge

4 Now, add an event-handler for the blue Ball sprite's CollidedWith event – an argument is automatically created

Don't forget

The Bounce method was described in the previous example and automatically creates edge arguments.

5 Snap statements into the CollidedWith event-handler to change the direction of each Ball sprite

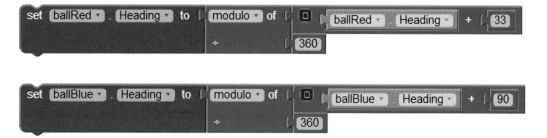

6 Run the app to see the Balls bounce around the Canvas and change direction when they collide with each other

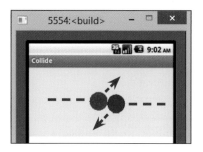

Hot tip

A procedure can be created to change the direction of multiple Ball sprites by passing in the current heading and returning a new value.

Dragging objects

When the user taps a sprite, a Touched event occurs and the sprite's Touched event-handler method can be called to perform an action. For example, to change a Ball sprite's PaintColor or to change an ImageSprite's Picture. The Touched method returns the XY co-ordinates at which the user has tapped the Canvas.

When the user drags a sprite, a Dragged event occurs and the sprite's Dragged event-handler method can be called to reposition the sprite accordingly. The Dragged method returns three sets of XY coordinates:

- **Starting Position** – the location on the Canvas where the user began this dragging action

- **Previous Position** – the location on the Canvas immediately prior to the current position

- **Current Position** – the location on the Canvas where the user is currently dragging the sprite

Assigning the XY co-ordinates of the current position to the sprite's MoveTo method enables it to move around the Canvas along with the user's dragging action.

Drag.apk

1 Start a new App Inventor project named "Drag" then add a Label, a Canvas, and a Ball sprite to the interface

2 Select the Ball component and set its properties to Enabled, PaintColor Red, Radius 20, Visible, X 0, Y 0

3 Launch the Blocks editor then add an event-handler for the sprite's Dragged event – arguments are automatically created

4 Snap in a statement to move the sprite to the current drag position

Beware

You must set the Ball sprite to Enabled or it cannot be dragged.

5 Snap in a final statement to display the current location

6 Run the app then drag the sprite to see it follow the current XY co-ordinates displayed on the Label

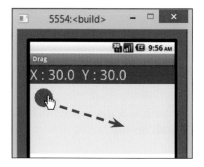 

Hot tip

Notice that the Ball sprite's Radius value is subtracted from the current XY position to center the sprite around that location.

Dropping objects

Dragged sprites can be made to disappear when they collide with another sprite to resemble the action of dropping an object into a recycle bin. Upon collision with another sprite, the CollidedWith event fires and can be used to set the dragged sprite's Visible property to false, causing that sprite to vanish.

Where multiple sprites appear on the same Canvas, their Z-index value determines which will appear uppermost when they overlap.

Drop.apk

1 Start a new App Inventor project named "Drop" then add a Canvas, a Ball sprite, an ImageSprite, and a Button component to the interface

```
                                    9:48
Drop


      ●

                   ▣


                             ♻


 Restore
```

2 Set the Ball sprite properties as in the previous example – so it becomes draggable

Don't forget

The Ball sprite Enabled property must be set to make it draggable.

3 Use the Upload File button in the Media column to specify an image resource for the ImageSprite

Media

bin.png

Upload File ...

4 Set the Ball sprite's Z property to 2 and the ImageSprite's Z property to 1 – to keep the Ball on top

5 Launch the Blocks editor then add an event-handler for the Ball sprite's Dragged event as in the previous example

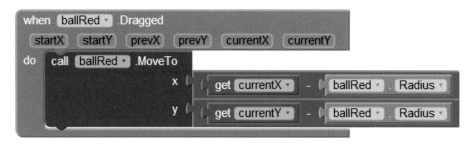

6 Add event-handlers for the Ball's CollidedWith event and for the button's Click event

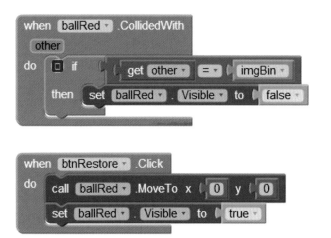

The CollidedWith event-handler tests that the collision occurs with the ImageSprite by comparing the <u>value</u> of the other sprite against its <u>component</u> identity.

7 Run the app then drop the Ball on the ImageSprite to see it vanish, and click the Button to see it reappear

The Ball sprite's Enabled property could also be toggled from true to false to disable it when invisible.

Summary

- The Player component on the Media components palette can be used to playback an app's audio files

- The Video Player component on the Media components palette can be used to playback an app's video files

- Audio and video files are added to an app as a Media resource in much the same way that images are added to an app

- The Camera component on the Media components palette can interact with the phone's camera interface

- Photos taken with the Camera component's TakePicture method get added to the phone's gallery like other photos

- The ImagePicker component on the Media components palette can select an image from the device's gallery

- Multiple screen apps have separate Blocks editor instructions for each individual screen

- A Ball sprite is a filled disc that resembles a ball, whereas an ImageSprite component displays a specified image

- Sprites must be contained within a Canvas component and can be animated by specifying their Speed, Interval, and Heading

- When a sprite hits the edge of the Canvas an EdgeReached event occurs that numerically recognizes that edge

- The edge value returned by the EdgeReached method can be passed to the Bounce method to reverse the sprite's heading

- The CollidedWith event returns the identity of the other sprite with which it has collided

- When the user taps a sprite, a Touched event occurs

- Dragging a sprite returns its XY coordinates which can be assigned to its MoveTo method so it follows the user's action

- Setting a sprite's Visible property to false causes it to disappear

8 Sensing conditions

This chapter demonstrates how an app can interact with an Android device's interfaces to sense its condition and utilize its social data.

Pin-pointing location

The App Inventor Sensors palette provides a LocationSensor component that can detect the phone's location using a combination of Wi-Fi, carrier network, and GPS techniques. A LocationSensor component is not visible on the app interface but has a LocationChanged method to return the current latitude, longitude, and altitude if supported by the device. It also has a CurrentAddress property, to extract the current street location from the co-ordinates, and a ProviderName property to specify a detection technique – "GPS" for phones or "network" for WiFi.

Geolocation.apk

1 Start a new App Inventor project named "Geolocation" then add three Labels and two Button components

Geolocation	🛜⏲ 🔋 9:48
WiFi Trace	GPS Trace

2 Add a LocationSensor component from the Sensors palette then check its Enabled property to make it active

Non-visible components

LocationSensor1

Properties

LocationSensor1

DistanceInterval
0 ▼

Enabled
☑

TimeInterval
60000 ▼

3 Launch the Blocks editor then add an event-handler for the first button's Click event to specify a detection type and Text

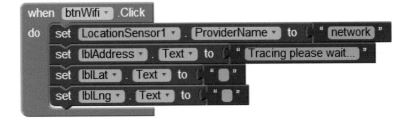

```
when btnWifi .Click
do   set LocationSensor1 . ProviderName to " network "
     set lblAddress . Text to " Tracing please wait... "
     set lblLat . Text to " "
     set lblLng . Text to " "
```

4 Drag in a call to the LocationSensor's LocationChanged method to display location details once retrieved by the detection type – arguments are automatically created

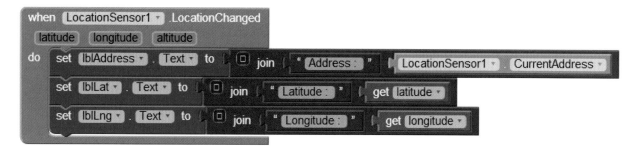

5 Add an event-handler for the second button's Click event to specify a different detection type and Text

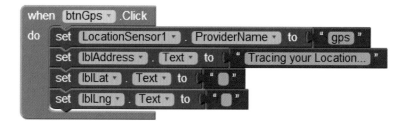

App Inventor cannot presently emulate LocationSensor apps – they must be installed on a device to run.

Beware

6 Install the app on your device, as described on pages 22-23, then run the app to discover current location

Recognizing orientation

The App Inventor Sensors palette provides an OrientationSensor component that can detect the device's current orientation.

An OrientationSensor component is not visible on the app interface but has an OrientationChanged method that returns three values expressed in degrees.

- **Azimuth** – the device's relationship to magnetic North, where 0° is North, 90° is East, 180° is South, 270° is West, etc.

- **Pitch** – the device's angle top-to-bottom, where 0° is level, increasing to 90° degrees as the device's top is pointed down, and decreasing to -90° as its bottom is pointed down

- **Roll** – the device's angle left-to-right, where 0° is level, increasing to 90° degrees as the device's left side is pointed down, and decreasing to -90° as its right side is pointed down

The values returned by the OrientationSensor have several decimal places but it is often useful to round them to whole numbers.

Orientation.apk

1 Start a new App Inventor project named "Orientation" then add three Label components

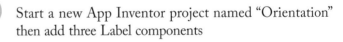

2 Add an OrientationSensor component from the Sensors palette then check its Enabled property to make it active

Properties

OrientationSensor1

Enabled
☑

Non-visible components

OrientationSensor1

3   Drag in a call to the OrientationSensor's
    OrientationChanged method to display orientation details
    as the device moves – arguments are automatically created

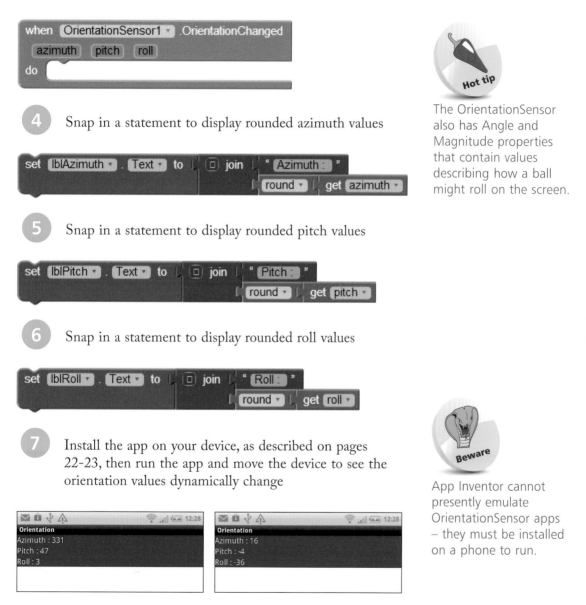

4   Snap in a statement to display rounded azimuth values

5   Snap in a statement to display rounded pitch values

6   Snap in a statement to display rounded roll values

7   Install the app on your device, as described on pages
    22-23, then run the app and move the device to see the
    orientation values dynamically change

Hot tip

The OrientationSensor also has Angle and Magnitude properties that contain values describing how a ball might roll on the screen.

141

Beware

App Inventor cannot presently emulate OrientationSensor apps – they must be installed on a phone to run.

Feeling movement

The App Inventor Sensors palette provides an AccelerometerSensor component that can detect the device's movement.

An AccelerometerSensor component is not visible on the app interface but has a Shaking method that is called when the phone gets moved vigorously in a shaking motion. This can be used to change an image source in response to the movement.

Acceleration.apk

1 Start a new App Inventor project named "Acceleration" then add a single Image component

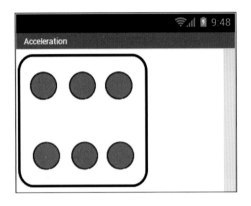

2 Use the Upload File button in the Media column to specify image resources for use by the Image component

Media
face1.png
face2.png
face3.png
face4.png
face5.png
face6.png
Upload File ...

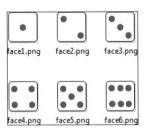

face1.png   face2.png   face3.png

face4.png   face5.png   face6.png

Properties

AccelerometerSensor1

Enabled
☑

MinimumInterval
400

Sensitivity
moderate ▼

3 Add an AccelerometerSensor component from the Sensors palette then check its Enabled property to make it active

Non-visible components

AccelerometerSensor1

4 Launch the Blocks editor then add an **initialize global** Variables block to store an integer value

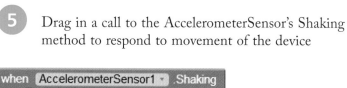

5 Drag in a call to the AccelerometerSensor's Shaking method to respond to movement of the device

6 Snap in a statement to assign an integer to the variable

7 Now, snap in a statement to assign the associated image number to the Image component on the interface

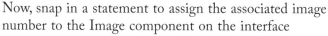

8 Install the app on your device, as described on pages 22-23, then run the app and shake the device to see the Image dynamically change

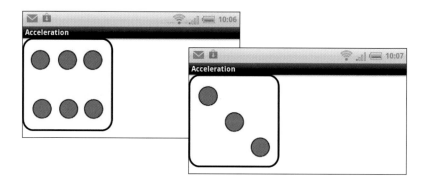

Don't forget

The Shaking method builds an image resource file name by combining "face", the random number, and ".png" – so this technique requires the image files to be named alike except for the number.

143

Beware

App Inventor cannot presently emulate AccelerometerSensor apps – they must be installed on a phone.

Picking contacts

The App Inventor Social palette provides a number of components to interact with members of your device's contact list.

An EmailPicker component is simply a TextBox component that automatically completes email addresses from your contact list. More interestingly, the ContactPicker component provides a Button on the interface that launches the device's contact list. Picking a contact fires the ContactPicker's AfterPicking event and stores that contact's relevant details in its ContactName and EmailAddress properties.

ContactPicker.apk

1 Start a new App Inventor project named "ContactPicker" then add two Labels and a ContactPicker component to the interface from the Social palette – the component provides a special button on the interface

Contact Picker	📶 🔋 9:48
Pick A Contact	

2 Select the ContactPicker component then check its Enabled property to make it active

Properties
ContactPicker1
BackgroundColor
■ Default
Enabled
☑

Don't forget

Like many other components, the ContactPicker can alternatively be enabled by adding a statement to the Screen's Initialize block to set the component's enabled value to true.

3 Launch the Blocks editor then drag in a call to the ContactPicker's AfterPicking method to perform an action whenever a contact has been picked

```
when  ContactPicker1 ▾ .AfterPicking
do
```

4 Snap in a statement to display the name of the contact that has been picked

```
set  lblContactName ▾ . Text ▾  to   ContactPicker1 ▾ . ContactName ▾
```

5 Now, snap in a statement to display the email address of the contact that has been picked

```
set  lblContactEmail ▾ . Text ▾  to   ContactPicker1 ▾ . EmailAddress ▾
```

6 Install the app on your device, as described on pages 22-23, then tap the ContactPicker button to open your device's contact list and pick a contact to see their details appear on the Labels

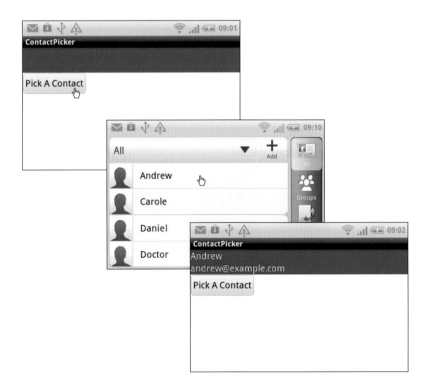

Hot tip

A ContactPicker also has a Picture property that stores the name of the contact's image file, which could be assigned to an Image component.

Calling phone numbers

The App Inventor Social palette provides a PhoneNumberPicker component that provides a Button on the interface to launch the phone's contact list – much like the ContactPicker described in the previous example. Picking a contact fires the PhoneNumberPicker's AfterPicking event and stores that contact's relevant details in its ContactName and PhoneNumber properties.

The Social palette also has a non-visible Phonecall component that can actually call a number. Its MakePhoneCall method dials the number assigned to its PhoneNumber property – which can be specified manually or by the PhoneNumberPicker.

PhoneCall.apk

A PhoneNumberPicker also has EmailAddress and Picture properties that store other details of the chosen contact.

1 Start a new App Inventor project named "PhoneCall" then add two Labels, a PhoneNumberPicker, and a Button, component to the interface

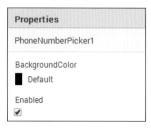

2 Add a PhoneCall component from the Social palette

3 Select the PhoneNumberPicker component then check its Enabled property to make it active

④ Launch the Blocks editor then drag in a call to the add PhoneNumberPicker's AfterPicking method to display details of the phone number that has been picked

```
when  PhoneNumberPicker1 · .AfterPicking
do   set  lblContactName · . Text · to   PhoneNumberPicker1 · . ContactName ·
     set  lblPhoneNumber · . Text · to   PhoneNumberPicker1 · . PhoneNumber ·
```

⑤ Add an event-handler for the button's Click event to assign the picked number to the PhoneCall component's PhoneNumber property

```
when  btnCall · .Click
do   set  PhoneCall1 · . PhoneNumber · to   PhoneNumberPicker1 · . PhoneNumber ·
```

⑥ Add a call to the PhoneCall component's MakePhoneCall method to make the phone call

```
call  PhoneCall1 · .MakePhoneCall
```

⑦ Install the app on your device, as described on pages 22-23, then tap the PhoneNumberPicker button to pick a contact's number and tap the Button to call that number

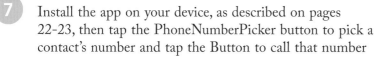

Texting messages

The App Inventor Social palette provides a non-visible Texting component that can listen for incoming SMS text messages when the app is running by setting its ReceivingEnabled property to true. Its WhenReceived event-handler then gets passed the phone number and message of incoming text messages.

The Texting component can also send SMS text messages using its SendMessage method. The Texting component stores details in PhoneNumber and Message properties. Its PhoneNumber property can be specified manually or by a PhoneNumberPicker.

Texting.apk

1 Start a new App Inventor project named "Texting" then add a TextBox, a PhoneNumberPicker, and a Button component to the interface

2 Add a Texting component from the Social palette

Non-visible components

Texting1

Hot tip

The PhoneNumber property can include hyphens, periods, and parentheses, but not empty spaces.

3 Select the PhoneNumberPicker component then check its Enabled property to make it active

Properties

PhoneNumberPicker1

BackgroundColor
■ Default

Enabled
☑

4 Launch the Blocks editor then drag in a call to the add PhoneNumberPicker's AfterPicking method to assign the phone number and message to Texting properties

5 Add an event-handler for the button's Click event then snap in a call to the Texting component's SendMessage method to send the message

```
when btnText .Click
do  call Texting1 .SendMessage
```

6 Snap a final statement into the Click event-handler to display a confirmation message to the user

```
set txtMessage . Text to " Message Sent "
```

7 Install the app on your device, as described on pages 22-23, and type in a text message, then tap the PhoneNumberPicker button to pick a contact's number and tap the Button to send the message

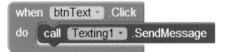

Tweeting updates

The App Inventor Social palette provides a non-visible Twitter component that can interact with the Twitter API to both send and receive status messages. In order to use this component the app must be given a unique name and registered for Open Authorization (OAuth) at **http://twitter.com/oauth_clients/new** Registration provides information required by the Twitter component's ConsumerKey and ConsumerSecret properties.

Once the ConsumerKey and ConsumerSecret properties have been set to those provided by OAuth the Twitter component's Authorize method can be called to open your account's log in page. After logging-in with your username and password an Authorized event fires and the screen returns to the app interface.

The Twitter component can listen for the Authorized event with its IsAuthorized event-handler and respond when it fires. After authorization, the Twitter component's Status method can then specify a Text value to submit to your Twitter status.

Hot tip

When registering the app, set the Application Website to your home page URL and set the application Permissions to "Read and Write".

APK

Tweet.apk

Beware

You must give your app a unique name and replace the XXXs shown here with your own OAuth ConsumerKey and ConsumerSecret.

1 Start a new App Inventor project named "Tweet" then add a TextBox, Button, and Twitter component to the interface

	📶 🔋 9:48
Tweet	

Logging in... Please wait

Update Status

Non-visible components
🄲
Twitter1

2 Launch the Blocks editor then add an event-handler for the screen's Initialize event and snap in statements to disable the TextBox, set account values, and Authorize

3 Add an event handler for Twitter's Authorized event to enable the Textbox and change its displayed message

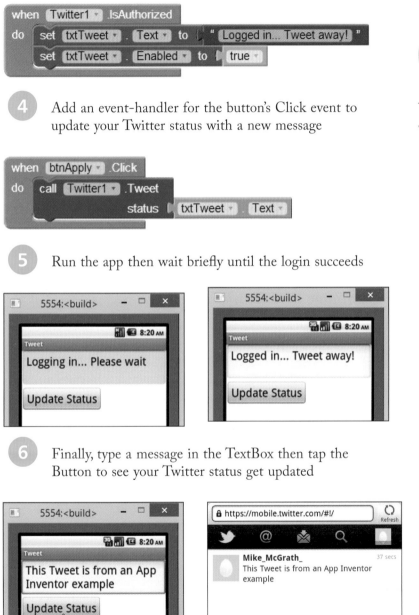

The Twitter component also has methods and properties to Search and Follow Twitter accounts.

4 Add an event-handler for the button's Click event to update your Twitter status with a new message

5 Run the app then wait briefly until the login succeeds

6 Finally, type a message in the TextBox then tap the Button to see your Twitter status get updated

Storing data online

A TinyWebDB component is a non-visible component that can dynamically store and retrieve data in an Android application. Unlike the TinyDB component, which stores data locally on the phone, the TinyWebDB component communicates with a Web service to store the data online – so the stored data can be accessed by multiple permitted apps and devices. The data must be assigned a tag name of your choice when it gets submitted by its StoreValue method. The data can subsequently be retrieved using that chosen name with its GetValue method.

TinyWebDB.apk

1 Start a new App Inventor project named "TinyWebDB" then add a Label, a TextBox, two Buttons, and a TinyWebDB component from the Storage palette

2 Launch the Blocks editor then add an event-handler for the submit button's Click event and snap in statements to store the TextBox content using a given tag name

3 Now, snap in statements to display the stored TextBox value then remove the TextBox content

④ Add an event-handler for the retrieve button's Click event and snap in statements to get the stored value using its given tag name

⑤ Add an event listener to assign the retrieved tag value – arguments are automatically created for its name and value

Don't forget

The **get** block is dragged from the **valueFromWebDB** argument on the **GotValue** block.

⑥ Run the application then enter some data into the TextBox and use the buttons to submit and retrieve content

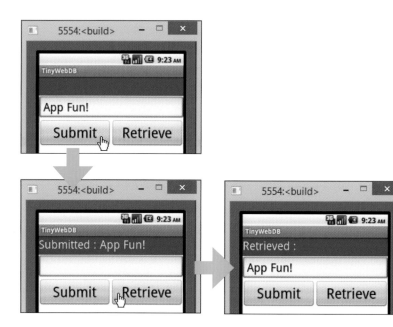

Beware

The default TinyWebDB service, used here for demonstration, is at **appinvtinywebdb. appspot.com** but is shared by all App Inventor developers so your data will eventually be overwritten. For actual apps you should create a custom web service – as described at **appinventor.mit.edu/ explore/content/custom- tinywebdb-service.html**

Summary

- The LocationSensor component detects the phone's location using a combination of Wi-Fi, network, and GPS techniques

- A LocationSensor's LocationChanged method returns the phone's coordinates, and its CurrentAddress property extracts the current street location from those returned coordinates

- The OrientationSensor component detects the phone's current directional and rotational orientation

- An OrientationSensor's OrientationChanged method returns values expressed in degrees for Azimuth, Pitch, and Roll

- The AccelerometerSensor detects the phone's movement and calls its Shaking method when the phone is moved vigorously

- The EmailPicker component is simply a TextBox that automatically completes email addresses from the contact list

- The ContactPicker component's AfterPicking method stores the contact details in ContactName and EmailAddress properties

- The PhoneNumberPicker's AfterPicking method stores contact details in ContactName and PhoneNumber properties

- The PhoneNumber component's MakePhoneCall method dials the number assigned to its PhoneNumber property

- The Texting component can listen for incoming messages when its ReceivingEnabled property is set to true

- A Texting component's SendMessage method sends its Message property to the number in its PhoneNumber property

- The Twitter component's IsAuthorized method fires when access is gained to a Twitter account, whereon its Status method can be called to update that account's status

- The TinyWebDB component has a StoreValue method to store data with a chosen tag name, and a GetValue method to retrieve stored data by specifying its given tag name

9 Deploying apps

This chapter describes the creation of an Android app from initial planning through to distribution.

Planning the program

When creating a new application it is useful to spend some time planning its design. Clearly define the program's precise purpose, decide what application functionality will be required, then decide what interface components will be needed.

A plan for a simple application to pick numbers for a lottery entry might look like this:

Program purpose

● The program will generate a series of six different random numbers in the range 1-49, and have the ability to be reset ready to make a new selection.

Functionality required

● A routine to generate and display a series of six different random numbers in the range of 1-49.

● A routine to clear the last series from display.

Components needed

● Six Label components to display the series of numbers – one number per Label.

● One Button component to generate and display the numbers on the Label components when this Button is clicked.
This Button to be disabled when numbers are on display.

● One Button component to clear the numbers displayed on the Label components when this Button is clicked.
This Button to be disabled when no numbers are on display.

● One Image component to display a static image – as decoration to enhance the appearance of the interface.

Omission of the planning stage can require time-consuming changes to be made later. It's better to "plan your work, then work your plan".

Toggling the value of a Button's Enabled property guides the user – in this case to reset the app before a further series of numbers can be generated.

...cont'd

Having established a program plan means you can now create the application basics by adding the components needed in Designer.

 1 Open App Inventor and start a new project named "Lotto"

Lotto.apk

 2 In Designer mode, add six Label components to the Viewer from the User Interface palette

 3 Now, add two Buttons and an Image component

The Screen, Label, and Button components initially display the illustrated default text – new text properties will be assigned in the next stage described overleaf.

Assigning static properties

Having created the application basics, on the previous page, you can now assign static values using the Properties column.

Lotto.apk
(continued)

1 Click anywhere on the Screen to select it then, in the Properties column, set the Screen's Title property to "Lotto Number Picker"

Properties
Screen1
Title
Lotto Number Picker

2 Select the Button1 component then, in the Components column, rename it to **btnPick** and in the Properties column set its Text property to "Get My Lucky Numbers"

Rename Component

Old name:	Button1
New name:	btnPick

Cancel   OK

Properties
btnPick
Text
Get My Lucky Numbers

3 Select the Button2 component then, in the Components column rename it to **btnReset** and in the Properties column set its Text property to "Reset"

Rename Component

Old name:	Button2
New name:	btnReset

Cancel   OK

Properties
btnReset
Text
Reset

Hot tip

The Label components in this program will have their Text property values assigned dynamically at runtime – no static properties are required.

4 Select the Image1 component then, in the Properties column, click the Picture property and click the Upload File button to launch the Upload File dialog

Properties

Image1

Picture

None	▲
	▼

Upload File...
Cancel   OK

5 Click the dialog's Choose File button to select an image file to upload for addition as a Media resource – this action also assigns it to the Image1 Picture property

Upload File ...

Choose File   lotto.png

Cancel   OK

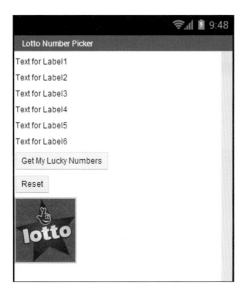

Don't forget

The project's Media resources are listed below the Components palette – the image file name gets added here.

Designing the interface

Having assigned static property values, on the previous page, you can now design the interface layout.

Lotto.apk
(continued)

1 Drag a HorizontalArrangement component, from the Layout palette, and drop it at the top of the Designer Viewer – above all other components

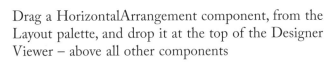

2 Select the HorizontalArrangement component then set its Width property in the Properties column to "Fill Parent" – so it fills the available screen width

3 Now, drag the Image1 component and drop it into the HorizontalArrangement1 component

You can set Width properties of the second Horizontal Arrangement and **btnPick** components to "Fill Parent" so they fill the available screen width – as shown here.

4 Next, add a second HorizontalArrangement component below the first one – then drop in the Button components

5 Add a Table Arrangement component into HorizontalArrangement1, to the right of the Image, then set its Width and Height properties to "Fill Parent", its Columns property to 7 and its Rows property to 3

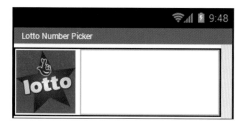

Properties

TableArrangement1

Columns

7

Rows

3

Visible

showing ▼

Width

Fill parent...

Height

Fill parent...

6 Drop new Label components into the left cell of each table row naming them **padTop**, **padMid**, and **padBtm** respectively, then remove their default text values

7 Set **padTop**, **padMid** and **padBtm** properties to a Height of 30 pixels and to a Width of 10 pixels – for positioning

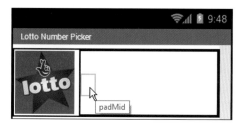

8 Edit the Text properties of the original Labels by removing "Text For Label" from each and changing their FontSize to 20 and Width to 30 pixels, then drop them one-by-one into the right cell of the middle table row

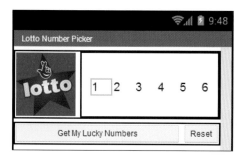

The padding technique is useful in Table Arrangement otherwise cell contents appear in its top left corner.

Initializing dynamic properties

Having designed the interface, on the previous page, you can
now add some functionality to dynamically set the initial Text
properties of the Label components and the initial Button states.

Lotto.apk
(continued)

1 Launch the Blocks editor then drag a **to** Procedures block
onto the Viewer and name it "Clear"

2 Snap statements into the procedure to assign an ellipsis
"…" value to each Label component in turn

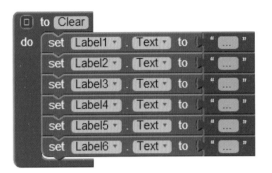

3 Now, snap in further statements to specify the Enabled
state of each Button component

4 Add an event-handler for the screen's Initialize event to
call the Clear procedure when the app starts

The initial value assigned
to each Label contains a
trailing space to separate
them when displayed.

162

The initial state of the app is determined by the blocks on the opposite page and it is desirable to allow the user to resume the initial state by resetting the app.

 5 Add an event-handler for the Reset button's Click event to call the Clear procedure when the button gets tapped

This app will use three variables to store numeric values when its Pick button gets tapped so these may now be initially defined.

 6 Drag an **initialize global** Variables block onto the Viewer and name it "nums", then snap in a **create empty list** block – this will store a list of randomized numbers

initialize global (nums) to □ create empty list

 7 Add an **initialize global** Variables block and name it "rand", then assign an initial value of zero – this will store successive single random numbers as the app proceeds

initialize global (rand) to 0

8 Now, add an **initialize global** Variables block and name it "temp", then assign an initial value of zero – this will temporarily store selected single random numbers as they get shuffled to ensure that no numbers are duplicated

initialize global (temp) to 0

Hot tip

You can collapse completed blocks in the Blocks editor by right-clicking on the block and choosing Collapse Block from the context menu that appears.

163

Don't forget

The **make a list** block creates an empty array that will be populated with items as the Pick button gets tapped.

Adding runtime functionality

Having created blocks to initialize dynamic properties, on the previous page, you can now add procedures to provide runtime functionality to respond when the Pick button gets tapped.

Lotto.apk
(continued)

 In the Blocks editor, drag a **to** Procedures block onto the Viewer and name it "Populate" – this will be used to fill the empty list variable with integer values

2 Snap a loop statement into the procedure to count from 1 to 49 – incrementing by one on each iteration

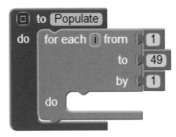

 Snap in a statement to assign the value of the counter "i" to the empty list variable on each iteration – filling the list with integers 1 to 49

 Drag another **to** Procedures block onto the Viewer and name it "Shuffle" – this will be used to rearrange the list's integer values into a random order

 Snap a loop statement into this procedure to count from 1 to 49 again, incrementing by one on each iteration

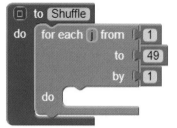

6 Snap in a statement to assign a random integer in the range 1-49 to a variable on each iteration

Notice that the counter variable in the second loop is named "j" to differentiate it from the first counter named "i".

7 Snap in a statement to assign the value of the list item at the counter "j" position to a variable on each iteration

8 Add statements to replace the list item values with others in the same range, but arranged in a random sequence and not repeating any single number

You don't need to understand in detail the algorithm that is used to shuffle the values.

Completing functionality

Having created procedures to Populate an empty list and to Shuffle the values it contains, on the previous page, you can now add a procedure to display six of the randomized list values.

Lotto.apk
(continued)

1 In the Blocks editor, drag a **to** Procedures block onto the Viewer and name it "Display" – this will be used to assign six list items to the Label components

2 Snap statements into the procedure to assign the value in list item one to Label number one, the value in list item two to Label number two, and so on

```
to Display
do   set Label1 . Text  to    select list item  list   get global nums
                                            index  1
     set Label2 . Text  to    select list item  list   get global nums
                                            index  2
     set Label3 . Text  to    select list item  list   get global nums
                                            index  3
     set Label4 . Text  to    select list item  list   get global nums
                                            index  4
     set Label5 . Text  to    select list item  list   get global nums
                                            index  5
     set Label6 . Text  to    select list item  list   get global nums
                                            index  6
```

Don't forget

After the values are displayed on the Label components the Pick button becomes inactive whereas the Reset button becomes active.

3 Snap in statements to toggle the state of each Button

```
set btnPick . Enabled  to   false
set btnReset . Enabled  to   true
```

4 Add an event-handler for the Pick button's Click event then snap in calls to the three procedures – to Populate the empty list, Shuffle its items, then Display six values

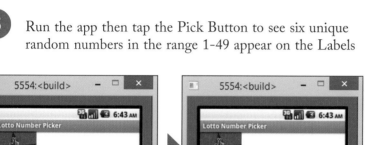

Hot tip

Procedure **call** blocks get added to the My Definitions drawer when the procedure is created.

5 Run the app then tap the Pick Button to see six unique random numbers in the range 1-49 appear on the Labels

6 Tap the Reset Button to see the series of six numbers get removed and the Button state resume readiness

Beware

App Inventor's Emulator is less responsive than devices so apps should be tested on as many actual devices as possible before distribution.

Distributing the application

Having worked through the program plan, on the previous pages, the components needed and functionality required have now been added to the app – so it's ready to be tested.

 Choose the Build > App menu option in App Inventor to download the app's APK package to your computer

 Connect your device to the computer then install the app on the device (as described on pages 22-23)

3 Launch the app to see that the Screen's Intialize event-handler has set the initial dynamic values of each Label and disabled the Reset button as required

4 Now, Tap the Pick Button to execute the instructions within its Click event-handler

A series of numbers within the desired range is displayed and the Button states have changed as required – a further series of numbers cannot be generated until the app has been reset.

Hot tip

Notice that no number is repeated in any series.

Make a note of the numbers generated in this first series for comparison later

 Tap the Reset button to execute the instructions within that Click event-handler and see the app return to its initial start-up appearance as required

You can adjust the font size, Button size, and and Label spacing, then test the app on several devices before distributing the app.

 Tap the Pick Button again to execute its Click event-handler code a second time

Another series of numbers within the desired range is displayed and are different to those in the first series when compared – Good, the numbers are being randomized as required!

 Now, restart the application and tap the Pick Button one more time

The generated numbers in this first series of numbers are different to those noted in the first series the last time the application ran – Great, the same sequence is not repeating on each run!

Selling your app

Having tested your app, as described on the previous pages, it can be distributed by forwarding the APK package file that gets downloaded using the Build > App (save.apk to my computer) option in the App Inventor menu. Other Android users can then install the app onto their device, just as you did for testing.

Your app may also be sold directly to users of other Android devices via the Google Play Store and via a number of third party "app stores". Sellers of apps on Google Play receive 70% of the selling price from the Google Checkout service with the remainder retained by carriers authorized to receive a fee for apps purchased through their network.

Submission of apps to Google Play is a relatively straightforward process that is lightly regulated.

 Open a web browser and visit the Google Play website at **play.google.com/apps/publish/signup**

 Sign in with your Google account, or create a new account, then accept the Developer Agreement

Google play

Not all countries are allowed to distribute Android paid apps due to Google Checkout restrictions but the list of allowed countries is constantly growing. The latest list can be found at **support.google.com/ googleplay/android- developer/table/3539140**

3 Pay the one-off $25 registration fee that enables you to publish software in the Google Play Store

4 Next, decide whether your app will be Free or set a price for your app in the range $0.99-$200 (0.50-100 GBP)

5 Now, choose "Upload Applications" in the Developer Console then provide the Upload Assets information:

- **Package** – the .apk file name of your app (maximum 50Mb)

- **Screenshots** – the look of your app (at least two are required)

- **High Resolution Application Icon** – a required high fidelity version of the launcher icon for your app (512 x 512 32-bit PNG)

- **Promotional Graphic** – to advertise your app in various locations on Google Play (180w x 120h 24-bit PNG)

- **Feature Graphic** – to advertise your app in the Featured section on Google Play (1024w x 500h 24-bit PNG)

- **Video Link** – to advertise your app on YouTube

6 Finally, provide the Application Information to make your app available on the Google Play Store:

- **Language** – the language of your app (default is US English)

- **Title** – the name of your app as you would like it to appear on the Google Play Store (one name is allowed per language)

- **Description** – the description of your app as you would like it to appear on Google Play (maximum 325 characters)

- **Application Type** – the type of your app (Application or Game)

- **Category** – the category group for your app (such as a News & Weather Application, or an Arcade & Action Game)

- **Contact Information** – the user support channel for your app as Website, Email, or Phone (at least one is required)

All prices and specifications are correct at the time of printing.

The average price of paid Android apps is around $3.00 – similar to the price of paid Apple apps.

The Google Play Store requirements may be subject to change.

Choose your app package name wisely – it must be unique and is permanent so it can't be changed later.

Summary

- A program plan should define the app's precise purpose, functionality required, and components needed

- The static properties of components, that DO NOT change when the app runs, can be set in their Properties column

- Images that are required to appear in the interface need to be uploaded for the app to use as a Media resource

- Horizontal Arrangement, Vertical Arrangement, and Table Arrangement components are useful for interface layout

- Label components with no text can be used for layout padding by specifying explicit Width and Height property values

- The dynamic properties of components, that DO change when the app runs, can be set to an initial value in their Properties column – or by the Screen's Initialize event-handler

- Changing the value of a component's Enabled property toggles its state between active and inactive

- Procedures can provide runtime functionality to respond to user actions in the interface

- The result provided when a runtime function is called can be displayed on a Label component in response to a user action

- An app should be tested on several devices before distribution to ensure it performs as expected

- Complete tested apps may be sold directly to users of other Android devices via the Google Play Store

- Submission of apps to the Google Play Store is a straightforward process that simply requires payment of a registration fee and upload of the app assets

+ Handy reference

This chapter describes the Built-in blocks you can use to build Android apps with App Inventor development.

Procedures blocks

The **to** block groups together a series of statements to be executed whenever that procedure gets called.

Optionally, **input** arguments may be specified for any **to** procedure block using its mutator button.

The **to result** block performs the same as a **to** block but additionally returns a **result** after executing its statements.

A **call** block is automatically generated for each procedure created so that the procedure can be invoked.

Variables blocks

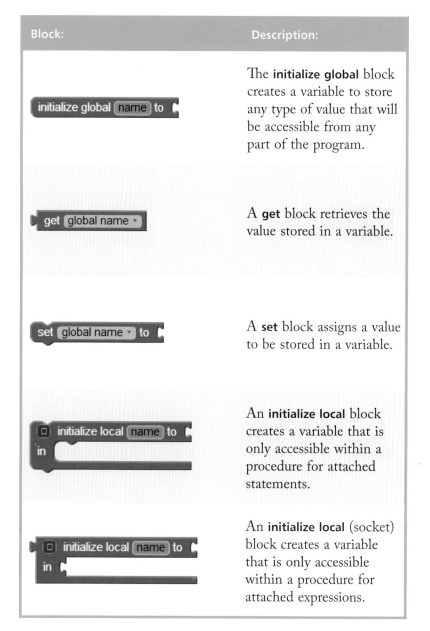

Block:	Description:
initialize global (name) to	The **initialize global** block creates a variable to store any type of value that will be accessible from any part of the program.
get (global name ▾)	A **get** block retrieves the value stored in a variable.
set (global name ▾) to	A **set** block assigns a value to be stored in a variable.
initialize local (name) to in	An **initialize local** block creates a variable that is only accessible within a procedure for attached statements.
initialize local (name) to in	An **initialize local** (socket) block creates a variable that is only accessible within a procedure for attached expressions.

Text blocks

Block:	Description:
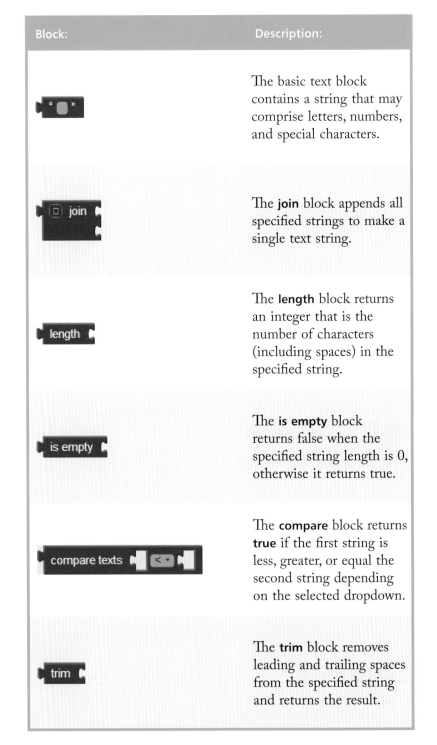	The basic text block contains a string that may comprise letters, numbers, and special characters.
	The **join** block appends all specified strings to make a single text string.
	The **length** block returns an integer that is the number of characters (including spaces) in the specified string.
	The **is empty** block returns false when the specified string length is 0, otherwise it returns true.
	The **compare** block returns **true** if the first string is less, greater, or equal the second string depending on the selected dropdown.
	The **trim** block removes leading and trailing spaces from the specified string and returns the result.

Block:	Description:
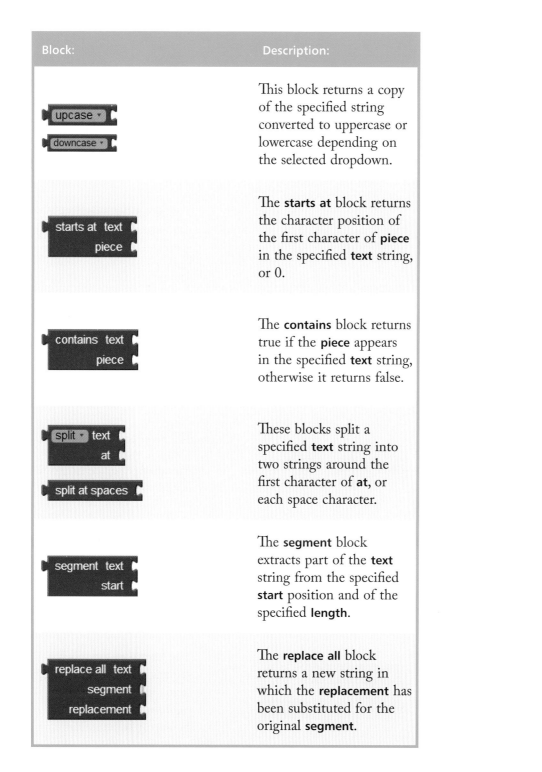	This block returns a copy of the specified string converted to uppercase or lowercase depending on the selected dropdown.
	The **starts at** block returns the character position of the first character of **piece** in the specified **text** string, or 0.
	The **contains** block returns true if the **piece** appears in the specified **text** string, otherwise it returns false.
	These blocks split a specified **text** string into two strings around the first character of **at**, or each space character.
	The **segment** block extracts part of the **text** string from the specified **start** position and of the specified **length**.
	The **replace all** block returns a new string in which the **replacement** has been substituted for the original **segment**.

Lists blocks

Block:	Description:
create empty list **make a list**	These blocks create an empty list or a list containing specified values in each list element.
select list item list index	The **select list item** block retrieves the value at the specified **index** position in the specified **list**.
replace list item list index replacement	The **replace list item** block replaces the value at the specified **list index** position with the **replacement** value.
remove list item list index	The **remove list item** block removes the item at the specified **index** position from the specified **list**.
is a list? thing **is list empty?** list	The **is a list?** block returns **true** if the specified **thing** is a list, whereas **is list empty?** returns **true** if the specified list has no items.
length of list list **pick a random item** list	The **length of list** block returns the number of items in a list, and **pick a random item** returns one randomly selected item.

...cont'd

Block:	Description:
	The **append to list** block adds one list to another, whereas **add items to list** appends single items to the end of a specified list.
	The **is in list?** block returns **true** if the specified **thing** is a **list** item, and **index in list** returns the index position of the specified **thing**.
	The **insert list item** block inserts a specified **item** at a specified **position**, and **copy list** returns a copy of a specified **list**.
	These blocks return the list as quoted comma-separated values with each row terminated by a CRLF character sequence.
	These blocks return the comma-separated row or table as a regular list of individual field elements.
	The **lookup in pairs** block returns the value associated with the specified **key** in a **pairs** list or the **notFound** default.

Control blocks

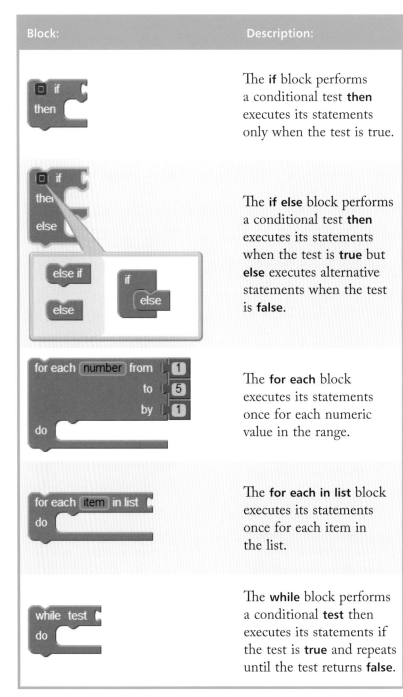

Block:	Description:
	The **if** block performs a conditional test **then** executes its statements only when the test is true.
	The **if else** block performs a conditional test **then** executes its statements when the test is **true** but **else** executes alternative statements when the test is **false**.
	The **for each** block executes its statements once for each numeric value in the range.
	The **for each in list** block executes its statements once for each item in the list.
	The **while** block performs a conditional **test** then executes its statements if the test is **true** and repeats until the test returns **false**.

Block:	Description:
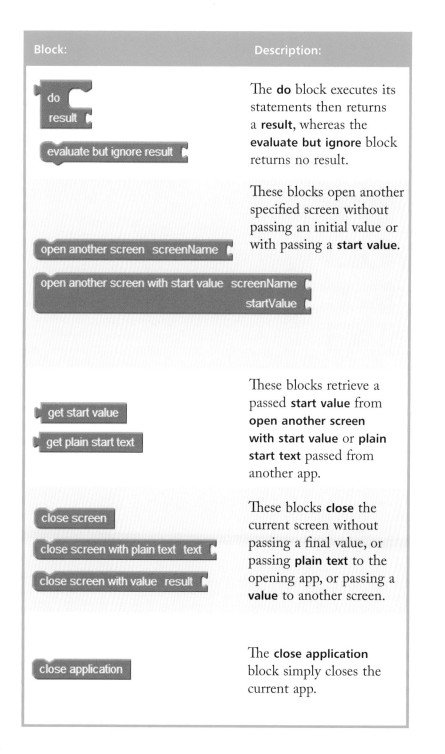	The **do** block executes its statements then returns a **result**, whereas the **evaluate but ignore** block returns no result.
	These blocks open another specified screen without passing an initial value or with passing a **start value**.
	These blocks retrieve a passed **start value** from **open another screen with start value** or **plain start text** passed from another app.
	These blocks **close** the current screen without passing a final value, or passing **plain text** to the opening app, or passing a **value** to another screen.
	The **close application** block simply closes the current app.

Math blocks

Block:	Description:
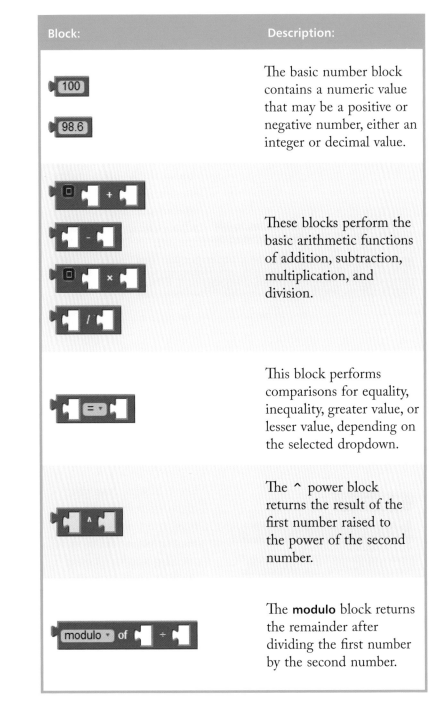	The basic number block contains a numeric value that may be a positive or negative number, either an integer or decimal value.
	These blocks perform the basic arithmetic functions of addition, subtraction, multiplication, and division.
	This block performs comparisons for equality, inequality, greater value, or lesser value, depending on the selected dropdown.
	The ^ power block returns the result of the first number raised to the power of the second number.
	The **modulo** block returns the remainder after dividing the first number by the second number.

Block:	Description:
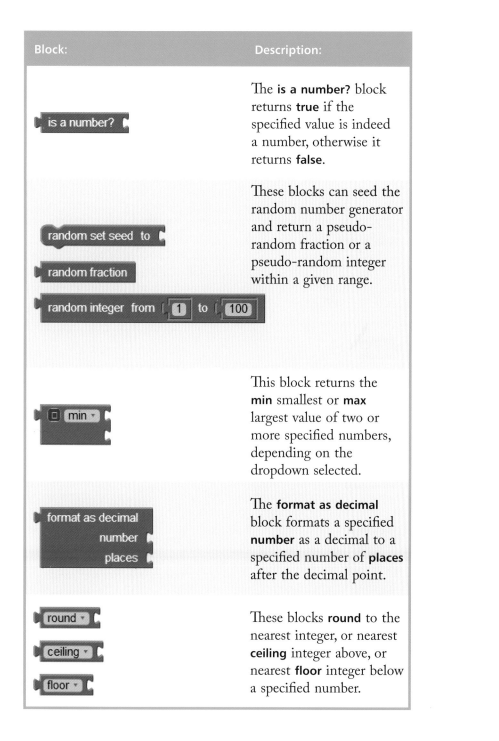	The **is a number?** block returns **true** if the specified value is indeed a number, otherwise it returns **false**.
	These blocks can seed the random number generator and return a pseudo-random fraction or a pseudo-random integer within a given range.
	This block returns the **min** smallest or **max** largest value of two or more specified numbers, depending on the dropdown selected.
	The **format as decimal** block formats a specified **number** as a decimal to a specified number of **places** after the decimal point.
	These blocks **round** to the nearest integer, or nearest **ceiling** integer above, or nearest **floor** integer below a specified number.

…cont'd

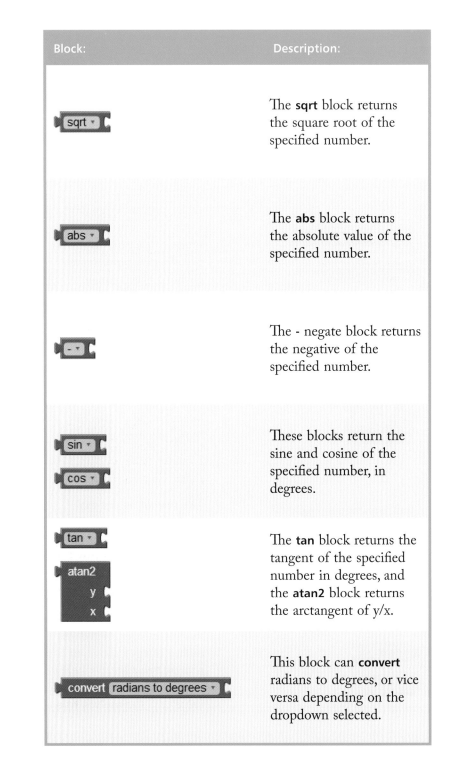

Block:	Description:
sqrt	The **sqrt** block returns the square root of the specified number.
abs	The **abs** block returns the absolute value of the specified number.
-	The - negate block returns the negative of the specified number.
sin cos	These blocks return the sine and cosine of the specified number, in degrees.
tan atan2 y x	The **tan** block returns the tangent of the specified number in degrees, and the **atan2** block returns the arctangent of y/x.
convert radians to degrees	This block can **convert** radians to degrees, or vice versa depending on the dropdown selected.

Logic blocks

Block:	Description:
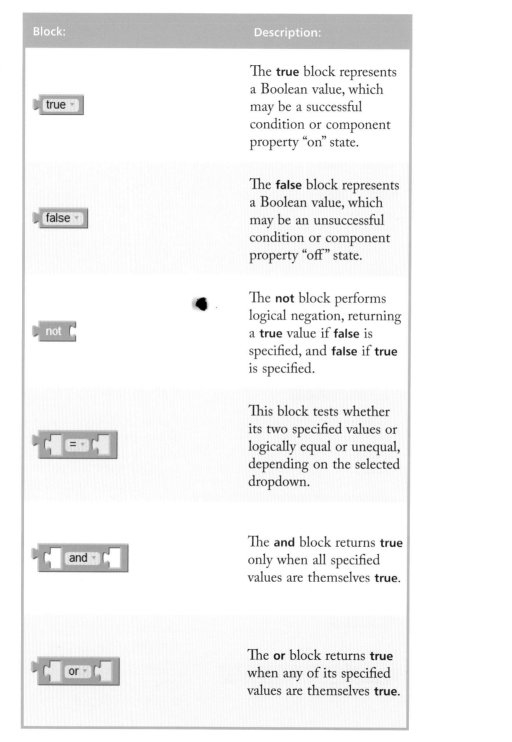	The **true** block represents a Boolean value, which may be a successful condition or component property "on" state.
	The **false** block represents a Boolean value, which may be an unsuccessful condition or component property "off" state.
	The **not** block performs logical negation, returning a **true** value if **false** is specified, and **false** if **true** is specified.
	This block tests whether its two specified values or logically equal or unequal, depending on the selected dropdown.
	The **and** block returns **true** only when all specified values are themselves **true**.
	The **or** block returns **true** when any of its specified values are themselves **true**.

Colors blocks

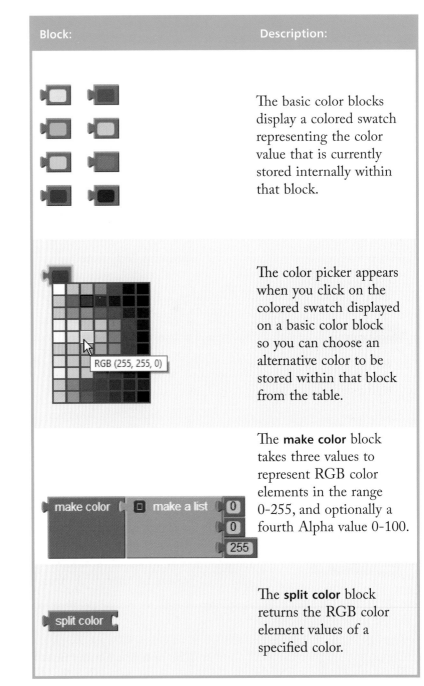

Block:	Description:

The basic color blocks display a colored swatch representing the color value that is currently stored internally within that block.

The color picker appears when you click on the colored swatch displayed on a basic color block so you can choose an alternative color to be stored within that block from the table.

The **make color** block takes three values to represent RGB color elements in the range 0-255, and optionally a fourth Alpha value 0-100.

The **split color** block returns the RGB color element values of a specified color.

Index